FOUL DEEDS AND SUSPICIOUS DEATHS IN THE WEST RIDING OF YORKSHIRE

TRUE CRIME FROM WHARNCLIFFE

Foul Deeds and Suspicious Deaths Series

Barking, Dagenham & Chadwell Heath
Barnsley
Bath
Bedford
Birmingham
Black Country
Blackburn and Hyndburn
Bolton
Bradford
Brighton
Bristol
Cambridge
Carlisle
Chesterfield
Colchester
Coventry
Croydon
Derby
Dublin
Durham
Ealing
Folkestone and Dover
Grimsby
Guernsey
Guildford
Halifax
Hampstead, Holborn and St Pancras
Huddersfield
Hull

Leeds
Leicester
Lewisham and Deptford
Liverpool
London's East End
London's West End
Manchester
Mansfield
More Foul Deeds Birmingham
More Foul Deeds Chesterfield
More Foul Deeds Wakefield
Newcastle
Newport
Norfolk
Northampton
Nottingham
Oxfordshire
Pontefract and Castleford
Portsmouth
Rotherham
Sheffield
Scunthorpe
Southend-on-Sea
Staffordshire and The Potteries
Stratford and South Warwickshire
Tees
Warwickshire
Wigan
York

OTHER TRUE CRIME BOOKS FROM WHARNCLIFFE

A–Z of Yorkshire Murder
Black Barnsley
Brighton Crime and Vice 1800–2000
Durham Executions
Essex Murders
Executions & Hangings in Newcastle
   and Morpeth
Norfolk Mayhem and Murder

Norwich Murders
Strangeways Hanged
The A–Z of London Murders
Unsolved Murders in Victorian and
   Edwardian London
Unsolved Norfolk Murders
Unsolved Yorkshire Murders
Yorkshire's Murderous Women

Please contact us via any of the methods below for more information or a catalogue.

WHARNCLIFFE BOOKS

47 Church Street – Barnsley – South Yorkshire – S70 2AS
Tel: 01226 734555 – 734222 Fax: 01226 734438
E-mail: enquiries@pen-and-sword.co.uk
Website: www.wharncliffebooks.co.uk

Foul Deeds & Suspicious Deaths in the West Riding of

YORKSHIRE

VIVIEN TEASDALE

First published in Great Britain in 2009 by
Wharncliffe Local History
an imprint of
Pen & Sword Books Ltd
47 Church Street
Barnsley
South Yorkshire
S70 2AS

ISBN 978 1 84563 095 9

A CIP catalogue record for this book is available from the British
Library.

Typeset in 11/13pt Plantin by
Mac Style, Beverley, East Yorkshire

Printed and bound in the UK
CPI Antony Rowe, Chippenham, Wiltshire

Pen & Sword Books Ltd incorporates the imprints of Pen & Sword
Aviation, Pen & Sword Maritime, Pen & Sword Military,
Wharncliffe Local History, Pen and Sword Select, Pen and Sword
Military Classics and Leo Cooper.

For a complete list of Pen & Sword titles please contact
PEN & SWORD BOOKS LIMITED
47 Church Street, Barnsley, South Yorkshire, S70 2AS, England
E-mail: enquiries@pen-and-sword.co.uk
Website: www.pen-and-sword.co.uk

Contents

Introduction and Acknowledgements

We all consider that the times we live in must be worse than previous times. We worry now about the number of 'feral' children, about the increase in knife crimes, the drunkenness on our streets and wonder what causes it and what to do about it. We use 'name and shame' to identify criminals, who once would have been put in the pillory. In the past, criminals were hanged in public on the 'Tyburn tree' at York, now marked by a stone near the racecourse. Later the hangings became private, carried out inside the prisons. The police force was developed from its inception in 1829 in London, throughout the country, its blue uniform and blue police station lamps gradually becoming part of society.

Tyburn Stone, York. The author

Yet looking back through newspapers over the past century, the same types of stories appear time and time again. Lawlessness and threats to society were of major concern. Their causes were considered to be the availability of cheap alcohol and a lack of 'moral fibre' on the part of the 'lower classes'. Modern newspapers reflect these same concerns – albeit expressed in less arrogant terms than the Victorian patriarchs.

Victorian police station lamp.
The author

The stories here cover a variety of incidents and outcomes, though the connecting themes are knives and alcohol. This was not intentional. It only became clear after I began to put all the stories together. It has been said that those who forget their history are doomed to repeat it, so perhaps now is the time for greater study of Victorian 'murder and mayhem'. It is certainly a subject of great fascination for most people, and perhaps we can learn something from it too.

Many thanks to the staff at many libraries and archives: Kirklees Library and Archives Services, Wakefield Library and Archives Services, Skipton Library, Leeds Library, Goole Library and Archive Service, Knaresborough Library, and Bradford Library and Archive Service for their unfailing willingness to help and offer advice on sources available.

Brian Elliott at Pen & Sword Books Limited has, as always, given invaluable assistance from initial idea to completed manuscript. My thanks also go to Bill Mathie at the School of Medicine, University of Leeds for his help in obtaining permission from the University of Leeds for the use of the Thomas Scattergood photograph on page 6 and Paul Stevenson and Richard Wade for their help in obtaining permission from the The British Postal Museum & Archive to use their photograph of a mail coach on page 151. All other photographs are from the author's collection. Maps are courtesy of the Ordnance Survey.

Family and friends have, as always, encouraged and supported me in bringing these stories to light, and I cannot thank them sufficiently.

CHAPTER 1

A Decade of Disturbances: The Yorkshire Chartists

I t is not quite a hundred years since the principle of universal suffrage became the norm in British politics. Prior to this, those with no voice in the running of the country had only one means of being heard. They rioted.

Early agitation for voting rights resulted in the Reform Act of 1832, but this had only been partially successful. The introduction of the Poor Law Amendment Act of 1834 brought greater hardship to those too ill to work and those simply unable to find a job. Poor harvests, economic downturns resulting in closure of many businesses, particularly in the north, brought many working families to the brink of starvation. It also seems to have brought about a new bout of political awareness.

By 1838 a national movement developed which became known as Chartism. It had six main aims, put together in the form of a Charter to which millions added their signature. The Chartists' demands were:

- The vote for all men over twenty-one.
- The introduction of the secret ballot instead of publication of votes, which led to intimidation by landlords and employers.
- The abolition of the property qualification for voting. The 1832 Reform Act had given the vote to men owning or renting property valued over £10. This excluded the majority of the working population.

THE ATTEMPTED REBELLION IN YORKSHIRE.

SHEFFIELD, THURSDAY EVENING.

Headline, Leeds Mercury, 1839. Author's collection

The European Situation, Leeds Mercury
1848. Author's collection

THE LEEDS MERCURY.

THREATENING ASPECT OF FRENCH
AFFAIRS.

THE LEEDS MERCURY.

THE SICILIAN INSURRECTION.

- A salary for MPs, allowing for the possibility of ordinary working men standing for Parliament.
- Electoral districts of equal size, instead of some areas with small populations being able to have the same, or in some cases more, MPs than the larger towns and cities.
- Annual elections.

None of these seem outrageous nowadays – apart from the last demand, they have all been introduced, the vote finally being extended to include all women in 1928 and the voting age reduced to eighteen in 1969. To those in power in the Nineteenth Century, the demands seemed to be the beginning of a revolution.

Revolution was a very real fear, probably greater than our current fear of terrorism. The French Revolution was within living memory and there were rumours of growing unrest across Europe, where 1848 proved to be cataclysmic. France, Germany, Italy, Austria and Hungary all suffered major disruptions and rebellions.

On 15 October 1838 a massive meeting was held on Hartshead Moor (then known as Peep Green), near Huddersfield, which was a central meeting point for the thousands who came from Leeds, Bradford, Huddersfield and Halifax. There was a fairground atmosphere, with whole

Headline, Leeds Mercury, *1838.*
Author's collection

"RADICAL DEMONSTRATION"
AT PEEP GREEN.

The "democrats of the West Riding," as they have dubbed themselves, had their field day, at Peep Green, on Monday last, to *demand, by petition,* the establishment of the Six Radical Points. We have told the Ultra-Radicals before that whatever might be said families attending, food and drink available and each group with bands and banners. Delegates from the West Riding to attend a National Convention to be held in London were chosen.

On 21 May 1839 a second mass meeting was held in the same place. Despite warnings from the magistrates, almost 30,000 people thronged the area, but the meeting remained peaceful, though there was a growing demand for more forcible action. By June there were signs that this had begun. In Barnsley, four men: Thomas Gomersall, James Frudd, a bank clerk, George Frudd, warehouseman and Abraham Newgate, shopkeeper, were arrested for 'drilling and training'. In August, Peter Hoey, John Widdop, George Uttley and John Vallence were arrested for 'attending unlawful meetings' and seventy-one rioters were arrested in Sheffield. Whilst ringleaders were usually tried and received prison sentences, many others were allowed (and encouraged) to plead guilty, then simply bound over to keep the peace, thus keeping them out of mischief for a short while, when it was hoped the disturbances would have died down.

The first Charter was presented to the Government in 1839, only to be rejected by Parliament. Serious riots broke out, particularly in the north. In January 1840 the troops were called out in Sheffield, setting up pickets on all the major roads. Police were fired on and attacked with sticks, bayonets and other weapons. By the end of the night:

> *... a great quantity of muskets, pikes, daggers, cats (an instrument with three prongs, which is meant to be thrown on the ground and destroy the horses' feet), powder, balls, grenades etc, were seized.*
>
> *The Times*, 16 January 1840

Further meetings took place around the town; leaders being brought in from further afield and more arms were found. It is no wonder that the Government was seriously alarmed. The Chartists too expected a revolution and were just waiting for the signal from the Sheffield group. As coaches from Sheffield arrived at each of the major towns en route – Barnsley, Bradford, Dewsbury – they were surrounded and the people

Perseverance Mill, Brighouse. The author

asked if Sheffield was 'up in arms' yet. In Dewsbury the whole town was taken over by armed men who ousted the six watchmen, including Matthew Hale, the inspector of the watch, who was fired at as he left. Over 200 men paraded around the streets and other villages in the area joined in the rioting. There were no troops stationed nearby that the local magistrates could call upon so the rioters were left to enjoy themselves for a while. In Bradford, military might was available to join the police and keep things under partial control.

For a while, peace existed but by 1842 the Chartists were ready to try again, with a second petition handed to Parliament. Again it was rejected and this time the more militant tendency prevailed. A general strike was called for and it was determined that the northern mills would be prevented from working by removing the plugs in the boilers. The series of events became known as the Plug Riots. In Halifax meetings were swelled by thousands coming from Bradford, Todmorden, Elland and surrounding areas. Troops were called out to guard the town and larger mills such as those of the

Ackroyd's. A mob of nearly 30,000, including thousands of women, marched into Halifax and up to North Bridge, where the Riot Act was read. Here they were charged by the police and quickly dispersed, only to regroup and go on to stop a number of mills around the town and in other villages such as Brighouse where skirmishes took place near the Perseverance Mill. Some of the prisoners were removed from Halifax to Wakefield, the magistrates then leading the soldiers up towards Salterhebble. Crowds, hurling stones, attacked them, fire being returned by the soldiers. Many on both sides were injured.

Other towns too suffered mobs attacking mills and stopping them working. Huddersfield, Cleckheaton, Brighouse, were inundated by the violent crowds before the police and troops finally regained control.

In September the assizes at York were faced with trying over 150 rioters. Many were allowed to plead guilty and be bound over, but others were sentenced to varying lengths in gaol – from a few weeks to a few months.

Though the movement seemed to have fizzled out, in 1845 a new aspect was added by the development of the Chartist Land Co-operative Society, which intended to buy land and lease it in smallholdings to members of the Co-operative. The following year saw the resurrection of the whole Chartist

Blackstone Edge. The author

movement, beginning with a meeting on Blackstone Edge, between Manchester and Halifax. Over 30,000 attended, listening to speeches from leaders such as Ben Rushton and Ernest Jones and renewing their commitment to political change.

Poor harvests in 1847–48 led to high food prices, trade depression led to mass unemployment and the third petition by the Chartists was again rejected by Parliament. Over 13,000 people gathered on Skircoat Moor near Halifax, along with the usual bands playing and groups marching in from surrounding areas. None of the principal Chartist speakers, such as Feargal O'Conner, editor of the *Leeds Northern Star*, the Chartist newspaper, appeared. The meeting ended peacefully.

Bradford area seems to have been the main hotbed of insurrection this time. In May 1848 the police arrested John Kilvington for riot and conspiracy. In immediate response, John Quin, Joseph Hollings, Thomas Bottomley, Henry Shackleton, Ralph Slater, John Smith, Isaac England, Thomas Whittaker, Edward Lee, John Taylor, William Smith, Christopher Moore, John Smith of Bingley and John Briggs attacked the constable, John Carruthers, and rescued Kilvington. All were later arrested and appeared before Mr Justice Erle. They were allowed to plead guilty and bound over to keep the peace.

At the end of the month a major battle erupted on the streets of Bradford. The authorities determined to arrest some of the local ringleaders – David Lightowler and Isaac Jefferson, also known as 'Wat Tyler' – 'a rabid speaker and man of ferocious aspect and Herculean strength'. Forty special constables set off to Adelaide Street, where the two men lived, but as the police arrived at the front door, the men escaped out the back. Almost immediately, a massive crowd appeared from the surrounding streets, attacking the police, throwing stones and beating them with pokers, sticks and fists. The police fought back and managed to win free but many were badly injured. News of the Chartists success spread rapidly and men surged onto the streets, soon joined by others from further afield. It was commented on that the men used carrier pigeons to send messages to others in Huddersfield, Halifax, Bingley

ALARMING CHARTIST OUTBREAK AT BRADFORD.

ARMING OF THE CHARTISTS IN YORKSHIRE.

Headline, Leeds Mercury, *1848.* Author's collection

etc to rally more men to the mob, something the Government had obviously not considered possible.

The magistrates responded by sending for even more troops and swearing in more special constables. Troops were moved all round the district, to the various towns to attempt to keep other areas under control, while in Bradford over 1000 police with troops assembled, while the crowd defiantly yelled insults at them. At 4 pm Superintendent Brigg marched his 1000 men from the Courthouse up Manchester Road, followed by 200 infantry with fixed bayonets and two troops of mounted Dragoons. They were determined to capture the ringleaders. No one attempted to stop them. Until they arrived at Adelaide Street, that is.

There they were met by a huge crowd, armed with anything they could lay their hands on. In the confines of the streets, the disciplined ranks were hampered and the police were soon driven back into the soldiers, who found it difficult to manoeuvre horses in the melee. The rioters lashed out at the horses' legs with staves, but the Chartists gradually gave way before the mounted men and fled through the narrow streets. Inns were ordered to close at 8 pm and the Riot Act was read so that the troops could act immediately if necessary. Though the two main ringleaders were not found the police did arrest William Sagar, who was later sent to York for trial for drilling, plus another seventeen men and also Mary, wife of Joseph Mortimer. Though the women are rarely mentioned in history books, they took an active part in the Chartist movement, raising funds and marching alongside the men. In many cases their verbal incitement was far worse than the men's. The *Wakefield Journal* of 1848, referring to Bradford, states:

On Monday evening a Meeting of Females was held in Peckover Walks, which was numerously attended; and the language made use of by the speakers, many of whom were females, was of the most obscene and disgusting character.

Map showing the courthouse, Bradford. Author's collection

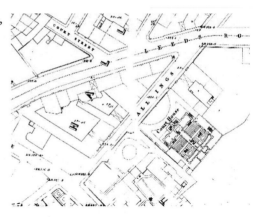

In September 1848 ten Chartists were brought before the courts, many witnesses being former Chartists themselves. Constable William Charnley of Bradford stated how he had been at Victoria Street and saw the prisoners, with fifty or so others marching in military order and obeying military style instructions such as 'Mark time', 'Halt' and 'Dismiss'. No attempt at secrecy was made in the drilling. The authorities were not above using a 'spy' system to obtain information and prosecutions. One of their principal witnesses was a man named Robert Emmett, an engine-tenter (engineer who was responsible for the boilers and engines of a mill).

Emmett had only lived in Bradford for the past six months, attending the meetings in Victoria Street where money was regularly collected in order to buy pikes ready for actions against the authorities. It was agreed that, in order to seize control of Bradford, they would blow up the Bradford Gas Works and kidnap the magistrates. They then arranged the group into a pseudo military order under a commanding officer (Emmett), with sergeants for every twenty-eight men, and corporals for every fourteen. Evidence suggested that there were forty or fifty groups or sections in Bradford, each one containing up to two hundred men. 'Sergeant' Wilson had managed to escape capture but 'corporals' William Wood and James Helliwell were among the prisoners. Another group were to destroy all the lamps in the town, plunging it into darkness.

Emmett's time in the witness box was enlightening to the jury. He agreed that he knew of a man nicknamed 'Skipton Dick'. In fact he was the man, having got the name because of a dog he'd had. No, he said, it was not he who had stolen some castings from a foundry in Skipton, nor was he the one discharged ignominiously from the army. He did admit he had been in Wakefield House of Correction though, for embezzlement and again for false pretences. The third time was when he was sent from Skipton Workhouse to Wakefield House of Correction for breaching their rules. Oh, and then he remembered he'd also been in there for desertion. Emmett had been married fourteen years, he said, and believed that his wife was in Australia. He was surprised to find she was living in Settle. He'd also gone through a 'marriage' with a woman in Ireland, but that didn't count because the 'vicar' was not a real priest, just someone 'with a gown pinned on him'.

The defence made much of all this, showing that Emmett was of such a bad character that nothing he said could be believed. Many of the other witnesses were Chartists too, turning Queen's Evidence to save themselves.

Despite this, the men were found guilty. The judge went on to say:

> *At that time there was a spirit of insubordination throughout the country approaching to rebellion, fomented by a number of foolish and wicked people. Had the objects they contemplated been carried out the country would not be fit to live in. It would be better to live under an absolute despotism with peace and protection for property.*

He obviously did not realise that, as far as many of the working classes were concerned, they already did live under that 'absolute despotism' since they had no say in their own government.

However, this was not the last of Robert Emmett. In December of the same year Benjamin Laycock, Francis Carmody, Paul Holdsworth and Martha Holmes were charged with having assaulted and robbed Emmett during the September riots.

Late one night, as Emmett had been returning home, he'd been seized by Laycock, egged on by Martha Holmes, who felt that he had plenty of 'blood money' on him. They tore his pockets open and robbed him of eleven shillings and four pence.

Emmett ran to the police, naming his attackers whom he said he knew well since he admitted he had helped drill and train them. The superintendent, Mr Collinson, gave him some money to find new lodgings since Emmett said he was too frightened to go home.

When the case came to court, Francis Carmody, who was only nineteen, stated that Emmett had, in fact, offered to train them, had offered to blow up the Bradford Court for three shillings, and had told them he was a deserter from the army. Emmett finally admitted that the money might have been lost during the scuffle rather than actually being stolen. His life history was again displayed for the jury, he had no witnesses to the events he said had taken place since no one would speak up for him, though hundreds were supposed to have seen it happen. The defendants were all described as 'quiet people' and respectable, despite which the judge told the jury that, if satisfied that an assault had taken place, they could find the prisoners guilty of that since it was not certain how the money came to be lost. The jury did as they were told and the judge passed sentence of two months' hard labour for each prisoner.

The Government had adopted a policy of spying, incitement, intimidation and harsh reprisals against those caught drilling or attending meetings. As the ringleaders were put in prison or transported the movement began to disintegrate and the riots died down.

CHAPTER 2

The Gamekeeper's Murder: Barnsley
1867

In December 1867, nineteen-year-old Harriet Thirkill was going home to Wortley. In the summer she had returned from her job as a house servant in order to attend the funeral of her mother, Mary. Now she was returning, not as might be expected for Christmas, but to attend the funeral of her younger sister. She was greeted with the news that local poachers had murdered her father, George. Not surprisingly, the girl collapsed and never fully recovered, ending her days in the asylum at Wadsley.

There had been a spate of poaching in the area – more than usual – so when gamewatchers James Hague, Thomas Oram and Thomas Mayes (also spelt Maize) knocked on Thirkill's door late on the night of Wednesday 11 December, George:

> *… although … engrossed by severe domestic affliction, his daughter lying dead in the house and his wife only recently interred, he deemed it necessary from information conveyed to him to accompany the underkeepers … to a place where it was understood the gang of poachers were.*

> Leeds Mercury

The place was the small village of Pilley, near Tankersley. In the field they saw two men with poaching nets. Thirkill immediately burst through the hedge, swinging his stout walking stick around him and shouting, 'What the devil are you doing here?' The men ran away, throwing stones at the pursuing gamekeepers. George was obviously quite fit for his age as he managed to catch one of the men and knocked him down, but the man got up and ran off across the field. One of the men had a dog, which was growling and barking at the gamekeepers, so Thirkill ordered Mayes to shoot it, which he did (it was later found injured, was treated and recovered 'in police custody'). He then told them to go after the man who could be seen running away, but took possession of the shotgun before Hague and Mayes set off.

They ran about a hundred yards but could no longer see the man. Wondering what to do next, they stopped and looked about. Turning back towards where they had left Thirkill, they heard a shot. They ran back. One man could be seen chasing gamewatcher Oram but three other men were standing over Thirkill, who was obviously badly injured from a gunshot wound. Hague ran to get help but by the time he returned Thirkill was dead.

The body was removed to Park House farm, owned by John Sykes, and the police sent for. Despite the late hour, Lord Wharncliffe and his steward both went to the farm to find out what had happened. The following day, Thirkill's body was taken back to his home in Pilley and laid beside that of his daughter.

The inquest was held at Park House farm on the following day. T W Wainwright, the surgeon, confirmed that there were no extensive marks of violence on the body, just the major gunshot wound to the abdomen which had killed the gamekeeper. The inquest was adjourned, meeting again at the *Wortley Inn*.

In December a £50 reward was offered for information which led to the arrest of the poachers and eventually suspicion fell on three men. Matthew Cutts, forty-two, a mason of Brightside, Sheffield, was a returned convict and had only just been released from prison. On the week prior to this incident, Cutts had appeared before Rotherham magistrates and fined fifteen shillings for poaching. Joseph Beardshaw (alias Beecher), twenty-six, of Carrbrook, Attercliffe, was a furnaceman and pot maker for the steel smelters. In 1865 he

Headline, Leeds Mercury, 1867.
Author's collection

THE MURDER OF LORD WHARNCLIFFE'S
GAMEKEEPER.
Yesterday the three men, Matthew Cutts, Joseph Beardshaw, and Joseph English were again brought before the Barnsley bench of magistrates, charged

had been tried at Leeds Assizes for poaching and been sentenced to three months in prison. The gamekeeper who captured him had been George Thirkill. The third man was Joseph English, thirty-three, also of Carrbrook, a carpenter. In 1861 he had been charged with the attempted murder of William Crookes in Ecclesfield. Although much of the evidence suggested that English, and his companion, Joseph Ibbotson, were involved it was insufficient for the jury to be absolutely certain, and English had been acquitted.

Constable Bennett of Sheffield police soon ran Cutts to ground. His landlady, Mrs Handley, immediately told the police that he had been home very late on the 11 December, whereupon Cutts admitted that he had been 'where the shot had been fired'.

Joseph English was finally tracked down by Detectives Samuel Hockaday and Wetherill to Tuxford, Nottinghamshire, where the police also found a gun buried in the garden. English admitted that the gun was his but on being charged with the crime replied, 'I know nothing about that.' Anne English, whose husband William was the half-brother of Joseph English, said that Joseph had arrived at her father-in-law's house in Tankersley late at night and 'put something down by the door'. After he left, she found nets and a gun. The nets were burnt and she buried the gun in the garden.

Beardshaw, who had been partly identified by the fact that it was his dog which had been shot and left in the fields where Thirkill had died, remained at liberty until 2 January 1868 when Superintendent Hall of Bradford arrested him at Littleborough, Lancashire. Beardshaw too immediately confessed that he had been poaching at Pilley, asking first if they had found his dog, then continuing:

> *I am not going to say I was not there, nought of the sort. I was there right enough, there's no use saying I weren't; of course they know that, they could tell by the dog.*

THE MURDER OF LORD WHARNCLIFFE'S
GAMEKEEPER.
CAPTURE OF TWO MORE OF THE GANG.

Capture of the Suspects, Leeds Mercury, *1867.* Author's collection

He also named his companions, though he denied any involvement in the shooting, saying he didn't even know anyone had been shot until much later. He agreed that the keepers had suddenly broken upon them:

They knocked me down and I acted dummy. They then began beating Gregory and I saw a chance of getting away and I got up and ran away.

At the subsequent trial, William Cliff, who had seen Beardshaw on the night in question and lent him £1 and a coat and cap, said that Beardshaw had also commented to him:

They shot my dog, and by God, Bill, if I had had a gun in my hand I would have shot the big b....r.

Beardshaw had then gone on to his mother-in-law's house at Clayton Heights in Bradford. He appeared to be unwell so she'd asked him why. He admitted to her that he'd been poaching and the keepers had attacked them, shooting his dog. The gamekeeper had knocked Beardshaw almost senseless and beaten his hands where he'd held them up to protect his head.

The case came to trial at the Spring Assizes in Leeds in April 1868 before Justice Hannen. Along with Cutts, Beardshaw and English, another man, Joseph Gregory, was initially brought to court under coroner's warrant but his defence argued that there was insufficient evidence to charge him with the murder. He had been so badly beaten by the keepers that he had been barely able to crawl home and, in fact, had been close to death himself. He was removed and later charged with poaching.

The court listened as the prosecution detailed the events of the night of 11 December 1867, showing Thirkill's dedication to his job. Thomas Oram gave further evidence of the shot being fired. He had been searching the man he had knocked down, finding he was armed with a stick and stones and already had a rabbit in his pocket. Three men then came up and one was armed with a gun. Oram called out to Thirkill, 'Look out, gaffer, they're here.' The man with the gun, turned and pointed it at Oram, who ran at him and knocked him down. The other poacher then picked up the gun. Someone shouted 'Shoot the b....r' and the man immediately shot Thirkill who was barely six feet away. It was impossible to tell whether the man had intended to shoot Thirkill or Oram as they were both so close.

Another poacher, who was in the ditch, then attacked Oram, who cried out for help from the other gamewatchers. As Hague and Mayes came up, the poachers ran away. Oram stated that Cutts was the man who had originally had the gun but dropped it when Oram had knocked him down. English had then taken up the gun and fired the shot. He was sure it was deliberate – the man had brought the gun up to his shoulder. It could not have gone off accidentally.

Henry Hoyland, a beerhouse keeper at Attercliffe, confirmed that English had left a gun with him. He had later given the gun to Cutts. Thomas Ellis, a publican from Ecclesfield explained how he and his wife had been returning home when they overtook Beardshaw and Gregory at the Floodgate near Ecclesfield Common. They had a dog with them and Ellis commented to them that if they had a hare left at the end of the evening, he would take it.

The defence then had their say. Initially Mr Blackburn raised an objection to the whole charge on the grounds that the keepers had no right to be in the fields anyway. The judge promptly overruled this, saying he had no doubts on that – the keepers had every right to arrest the men. He pointed out that the poachers, if they had taken their weapons with the intention of using them to prevent being arrested, would be guilty of murder. If, on the other hand, they had taken them purely in pursuit of game and only used them to kill Thirkill in the heat of the moment, then they would be guilty of manslaughter.

Defence argued that the evidence against the men was based solely on Oram's story. Mr Waddy, defending English, then went on to say that even if his client had been present, the charge should have been manslaughter, not murder, because of the misconduct of the keepers in rushing at the poachers and striking them 'without a word of challenge'. The prisoners, it was said, were unarmed (the stones were only for weighing down the nets, the sticks for killing game, not people) whereas the keepers had gone 'prepared for a conflict'. It was, he said:

> *not fair on the part of the prosecution to produce weapons which it was said the prisoners had used and not the four-foot bludgeons used by the keepers.*

As Mr Waddy finished his speech, cheers burst from the gallery and the judge ordered the loudest to be removed.

After his summing up, the jury retired and within half an hour delivered their verdict:

> Cutts and English were guilty of manslaughter; Beardshaw was found not guilty.

The judge, whilst pointing out that the jury had spared the prisoners the worst penalty, still felt that he had to pass

St Leonard's church, Wortley. The author

sentence 'which would act as a warning on those engaged in similar pursuits and in the use of weapons likely to lead to fatal results'. He sentenced English to ten years' penal servitude, whilst Cutts, who did not actually fire the gun, received five years.

Beardshaw, and Gregory who had originally been charged with being involved, were both tried for poaching. Breadshaw received eighteen months and Gregory fifteen months' imprisonment.

In January the furniture and goods from Thirkill's house were sold off by auction to raise funds for his orphaned children, four of whom were still living at home, the youngest being only seven years old. Lord Wharncliffe took over the care of the young children. Later the people in the village of Wortley raised funds to erect a tombstone at St Leonard's church in honour of the gamekeeper.

CHAPTER 3

A Starving Child: Barnsley 1870

At the *Wood Street Hotel*, Barnsley, the coroner heard one of the worst cases of neglect he had come across.

Abraham Rock, fifty-two, was a stonemason, as was his brother, Edwin. Abraham lived at 3 Court, Wood Street which was not a very well-to-do area, yet as well as his wage from his job he had some property which brought in an extra five shillings and sixpence – more than enough to feed and maintain his family.

In 1869 his wife, Sarah, died. From then on his eldest daughter, Ann, who was just thirteen, had to look after the other three children: George, Arthur and Benjamin, as well as run the house for him. He seemed to expect her to do so on nothing, rarely giving her money for food yet telling her she was not to ask the neighbours for anything as he didn't want others talking about him.

Ann sensibly ignored that and often resorted to asking neighbours for food or going to her older brother, Eli, where her sister-in-law frequently provided them all with a meal. She would not give them food to take home, as she had heard her father-in-law tell the children that if anyone gave them food they must put it in the swill tub for the pig. Ann often rose early to go to the waste heaps nearby, scrabbling amongst the dirt to find cinders and bits of coal in order to make a fire for the family. She also ferreted around in the swill bin to find

Headline, Leeds Mercury, *1870.*
Author's collection

A CHILD STARVED TO DEATH.

COMMITTAL OF THE FATHER FOR MANSLAUGHTER.

On Tuesday, an inquest was held at the Wood Street Hotel, Barnsley, before Mr. Taylor, on the bread, which was often the only food the children had all day. Some days there was not even that bit of sustenance and the children had only cold water to drink. Sometimes, when he had collected the rents, her father would give her the odd shilling to buy food, but more often said he had none. When the children cried for bread, he threatened to beat them. The rest of the money was spent on drink.

As times got worse, the family moved into the cellar of the house, living together in one damp room and sleeping in one bed.

The young girl managed to keep things going until the youngest, Benjamin, fell ill as a result of being in such a cold, damp room. She asked her father to get a doctor for the child, who was only two years old, but he replied, 'I'm stalled of doctors'. She consulted her sister-in-law, Sarah, who also asked Abraham to call the doctor but again he refused. She went to the relieving officer, Mr Wilkinson, asking him to call, but heard nothing further.

The neighbours, too, were concerned. Marie Harrison, who lived in the same yard and often provided food for the children also went to see Mr Wilkinson, asking him to come but to no avail. Wilkinson knew that Abraham was well able to maintain his family and, presumably, saw no reason to pay out parish funds unnecessarily. The most he did do was to give Marie a note for Abraham saying that if he didn't provide for his family 'he should take measures to compel him to do so'. Marie did not pass on this message.

Jane Butterfield, another neighbour, heard the child crying for food and heard Abraham reply that he would 'punch it to death if it was not still'. She also overheard Ann asking her father how they would manage to bury Benny if the boy died. The father simply swore at the girl and said he would throw the child down the well.

On Friday, 4 March, Sarah Rock took little Benjamin home to try and feed him, calling in Matthew Corr (or Corri), the surgeon's assistant, but it was too late. By Sunday, the child was dead.

On Monday, Constable Whittaker arrested Abraham Rock, charging him with causing his son's death through starvation and neglect. Rock replied that it wasn't true, he had been well provided for. At the later inquest the surgeon, Mr Blackburn, said that he:

> found the stomach exceedingly pale and the whole of the intestines to the anus empty, containing neither the remains of food or faecal matter. There was not a trace of fat in the abdomen or on any part of the body. It was the worst case of emaciation he had seen in his practice.

In his opinion, the cause of death was:

> want of nourishment, with pleuro-pneumonia, but the latter might have been cured or relieved by food.

The coroner's jury returned a verdict of manslaughter against Abraham Rock and sent him for trial at the next assizes.

At the trial, in Leeds, the evidence was put before the court, this time including the fact that Abraham Rock had in the past tried to hang himself.

The defence declared that the police had 'the wrong man in the dock'. In his view, the culprit was the relieving officer who had failed to visit the child on a number of occasions and offered them no help, despite the doctor's assistant, Mr Halton, sending a note to the relieving officer to provide food. The judge disagreed, saying that since Rock was living in his own property, rent free, and had the income from the other properties, it was not up to the parish to provide relief for his children.

The jury lost little time in finding the father guilty of neglect. In sentencing him to five years' imprisonment, the judge told him:

> You are unfit evidently to be the protector, the guide and the example of your family and I cannot help thinking that their loss will be as little felt by you as your loss will be felt by them.

The following month Mr Wilkinson, the relieving officer who should have dealt with the case, was brought before an investigating committee to answer a charge of neglect. Mr Tyas, the clerk, had received a letter from the Poor Law Board referring to the comments in the *Leeds Mercury* and asking for an investigation.

The women went through all their evidence again, showing how they had contacted the relieving officer over a period of weeks prior to the child's death, but no aid had been given nor had Wilkinson even been to visit the household. Dr Blackburn had eventually been called in by Sarah Rock, who had had to agree to pay any medical fees.

In his defence, Wilkinson said that he knew Abraham Rock had sufficient means to pay for his family and that Rock, when tackled on the subject, had told him the family were well cared for. Wilkinson pointed out that if he had intervened, paid an allowance and brought Rock before the courts it was probable that the case would have been thrown out since Rock was not destitute and Wilkinson would have had to pay the costs himself.

The committee finally decided that it was just 'an error of judgement' but that Wilkinson should not have been satisfied with the word of the 'offending person' as to the welfare of the children.

CHAPTER 4

Determined Attempt to Murder: Batley Carr 1863

Sarah Ann Dewhirst had had enough. For a number of years she had lived with James Stephens in Batley Carr but she, and her twenty-three-year-old daughter, Emma Bottomley, were thoroughly fed up with his 'bad conduct' – drinking mostly. They threw him out of the house, much to his annoyance and he vowed that 'he would take both their lives and then destroy himself'.

On Thursday evening, 12 March, Sarah Ann went to visit one of her neighbours, Edward Owen on Lydgate Lane. Stephens heard of this and set out there too. So did the daughter, intending to warn her mother in case Stephens intended 'some mischief'.

Emma reached the house but had hardly walked through the door when Stephens rushed at her, stabbing her in the thigh with a knife. As she cried out, 'Oh, mother, he has stabbed

Map of Lydgate Lane, Batley Carr. Author's collection

me,' he struck again, inflicting a deep wound just below her left breast.

Sarah Ann grabbed hold of Stephens and dragged him off her daughter, being stabbed in her arm as she did so. Stephens eventually fled the scene and managed to evade the police search that was immediately begun for him.

Dr Rhodes of Batley Carr and Dr Thornton were both called in to look after Emma. There was so much blood soaking her clothes and seeping out onto the floor that at first it was thought the femoral artery had been cut, but this proved not to be the case.

On the Friday morning, Stephens strolled in to the local police station and calmly asked what he was wanted for. Superintendent Thomas immediately charged him with attacking the girl. Stephens simply remarked, 'Oh, the two who are going to swear against me this time have done so before.' He was then taken to Dewsbury lock up and appeared before the magistrates there on Monday morning. Unfortunately, it proved impossible to hear the case because the doctors were still so worried about Emma's condition that she was not able to attend court to give evidence against him. There was still uncertainty as to whether she would recover or whether the final charge would be murder, so the case was put back a week.

The following week the case was heard, Emma having recovered sufficiently to attend. Alderman Scholes prosecuted whilst Stephens conducted his own questioning of the witnesses.

On the Saturday prior to the attack, Stephens had gone to Sam Healey's house, where Sarah Ann and her daughter lodged. He had asked for both women, but Sam had insisted they were out. Stephens was heard to make threats against them both, which was why Emma had rushed off to warn her mother on the evening of the attack.

Sarah Ann told the court how her daughter had come to Owen's house, but had barely got to the door when Stephens arrived. 'Sarah Ann, come here,' he'd shouted but she'd replied, 'I've said I will not go out to you any more.' Her daughter had repeated this to Stephens, whereupon he'd roared out, 'Willn't she!' and rushed in, attacking Emma, and swearing at her, 'You rotten whore, I'll stab thee.'

Alderman Scholes asked Sarah Ann what had happened next. She'd seen the knife and flung Stephens towards the door, where he landed half in and half out. Owens arrived and fell on top of Stephens, who pushed him away and fled, leaving his cap and 'wrapper' behind.

It was then Stephens turn to ask the questions.

'Did we not walk comfortably together?' he asked, referring to a meeting earlier that day.

'Yes,' Sarah Ann admitted, 'from the Knottingley Wells.'

'Didn't you agree to come out with me?'

'No, I said I'll not come out with you for your drunken ways. I'm stalled of thee.'

'You are the wife of Joseph Dewhirst?'

'Yes.'

'Were you not married to John Mattall in Leeds?'

'What's that got to do with it?' Sarah Ann asked, perplexed.

'Isn't he still alive?'

The Bench immediately ruled that she need not answer the question and very sensibly she didn't. Stephens then continued.

'Didn't you strike me with a poker when we was living at Kiln Croft?'

Sarah Ann turned to the Bench for help, but this time they decided she had to answer. The question and answers continued:

'Haven't you threatened to open my skull?'

'Doesn't matter if I have or not!'

'Yes, it does. Haven't you threatened to cut my throat?'

'No, never.'

'When I went away didn't you come after me?'

'When was that?'

'Two years since.'

The Bench again intervened to say this all had no bearing on the case, but the two combatants were squaring up to each other and continued:

'Have you not frequently come to my lodging when I've been in and wanted me to agree to go together again?'

'Yes, and thou's come to me so there's nowt in that.'

'Have you ever come to my lodgings at Kiln Croft at late hours of the night and wanted to get in to me?'

'Yes, and thou's come to me on't same errand!'

The court erupted in laughter and Sarah Ann's evidence came to an end.

Emma Bottomley then came into the court, looking pale and weak. She was offered a small glass of wine before she gave evidence to Alderman Scholes. Stephens initially said he 'didn't want to hurt her by talking as she seems very weak but I'll ask one or two questions', going on to get her to confirm that he had not used any bad language to her on the night in question, but also asked:

'Was you not about a yard outside the door when you pulled the wrapper off my head?'

'I did not touch you. I did not get outside the door before I was stabbed.'

At the end of the questioning, Emma bravely asked to stay in court as she 'wanted to see the case through'.

Edward Owens confirmed Emma's statement that both women were inside the house and Stephens had deliberately rushed in at them, though he didn't see the actual stabbing. Stephens then suggested to him that it was Sarah Ann who had pushed her daughter down but this was denied. Next Stephens suggested that Priscilla, Owens' 'woman' had pushed Sarah Ann into him (Stephens) but this too was denied: 'Not a bit of it' was the reply from Owens.

Sam Healey then explained his part in the affair. He had seen Stephens prior to the attack when the man was drunk and 'kicking up a row', threatening to murder him if Healey didn't turn the women out of his house. On the Monday before the attack, he'd seen Stephens approaching the house, so had hidden himself near the fire, which provided the only light in the room. Stephens had opened the door, looked round and called out for Sarah Ann then gone away again.

DETERMINED ATTEMPT AT MURDER AT BATLEY CARR, NEAR DEWSBURY. *Headline,* Leeds Mercury, *March 1863.* Author's collection

On the Thursday, he'd seen Emma set off for Owens' house to warn her mother and followed, arriving too late to witness the attack but saw Emma covered in blood and ran for the police.

Sergeant Miller of the Borough police arrived at the scene around twenty past eight, seeing Emma lying in a pool of blood and noting the extent of the wounds as she was undressed and put to bed. He collected both her clothes and the ones Stephens had left behind. Stephens acknowledged that the wrapper was his.

Superintendent Thomas confirmed that he had visited Stephens' house and also searched his trousers, finding a double bladed pocketknife 'of large dimensions' in one pocket. Both blades had recently been sharpened. Stephens asked him:

'Was I drunk or sober when I called [at the police office]?'

'You appeared to have been drinking.'

Stephens seemed satisfied, asking nothing more, even when cautioned. His question on cross-examination were considered 'shrewd' – he had tried to discredit the main witness against him, Sarah Ann, and would later use Superintendent Thomas's comments in the trial at York Assizes.

The local newspaper described the protagonists, saying Stephens was of 'low stature' and that Mrs Dewhirst (alias Nuttall) was:

'very tall, and not ill looking; about forty-five years. The daughter is of equal height, about twenty-six.'

Both were textile workers, employed at Company Mill, Batley Carr Road.

The newspaper also commented that:

'The evidence disclosed that several persons were living in adultery together apparently without the slightest shame', which seemed to be more offensive to the editor than the wounding.

At York, Stephens's defence, which he conducted himself, was that he was intoxicated and didn't know what he was doing. He had a knife in his hand because he had been cutting nuts. If he had struck at Emma Bottomley, which he did not remember, it was accidentally and under the exasperation of the moment.

The jury were sufficiently swayed to find him guilty of wounding with intent to do grievous bodily harm, rather than with intent to murder. The judge still sentenced him to ten years' penal servitude.

CHAPTER 5

Manslaughter of Samuel Land: Batley 1863

There was great difficulty in prosecuting Michael Egan for the manslaughter of Samuel Land, though prosecuting William Simpson presented no difficulty. Mr Kydd, who was defending Egan, was unable to communicate effectively with his client so a satisfactory plea could not easily be obtained. Michael Egan was totally deaf, and in the nineteenth century this usually meant the sufferer was unable to speak properly too. By means of signs, Egan was eventually able to understand what was required and a plea of not guilty entered.

Michael Egan, twenty-seven, lived with his brother John, and his family in Wood Well, Batley. The brothers, and their mother, who lived there too, all came from Ireland, finding work doing general labouring and 'navvying'. Michael, like many other navvies in the area at the time, was employed by Bray, a railway contractor, and had been working there for four months. Unfortunately, as the local newspaper said:

Navvies are not the most gentle of human beings and when in a 'sportive' mood at work had sometimes seized on Egan as a 'make-sport' and plagued him very much. On some of these occasions his passion had risen to a fearful height and he has generally quietened his tormentors by seizing a shovel and showing them by signs that if they didn't leave him he would cut off one of their heads with the instrument and kick it high in the air.

A MAN KILLED BY A NAVVY, AT BATLEY. *Headline,* Leeds Mercury, *June 1863.* Author's collection

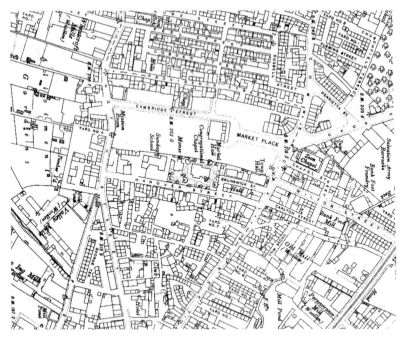

Map of Commercial Street, Batley. Ordnance Survey

Not surprisingly after such treatment, the severely disabled man was often 'sullen and moody'. He developed a reputation as a 'fighting man ... determined and naturally quarrelsome'. He found that his fists could earn him some respect and 'was often at the service of beerhouse keepers who wanted to clear a disorderly house'.

On 20 June, a Saturday, Egan went, with some other Irishmen, to the *Old House at Home* a beerhouse on Commercial Street, Batley. The inn fronted onto Commercial Street with an entrance door more or less level with the pavement but at the side was a ginnel, which sloped down to where there was another door. Through this door were three steps up into a long, narrow room with a bar at one end and a small stage at the other. The stage had been constructed by knocking down the partition wall and inserting a window that overlooked the street. There were steps up to the stage and others leading down to the kitchen area. Egan and his friends had been drinking in the kitchen, but they then decided to go to the upstairs room. There they found a number of men all seated round the bar, including Samuel Land, twenty-six, who was a weaver working for Thomas Lee of Soothill, a blanket manufacturer, and William Simpson, twenty-nine, a brickmaker who had been working for J Blackburn, brick manufacturer.

During the evening, Simpson bragged that Egan could fight any man in Batley, to which Land replied that he could find a man to fight him. Egan was not sure what was going on but understood that it involved a fight, so jumped up and 'throwing himself into a fighting attitude, offered to set to with Land'.

Land refused so Egan sat down again. Some time later, Simpson place five shillings (25p) on the table as a bet in favour of Egan against anyone else. Again, Egan jumped up ready to fight, but again he was calmed down by Ann Chappell, the landlord's wife.

Land then tried to leave the inn to escape any more aggression, but Simpson urged Egan on to stop him. Egan struck Land on the shoulder at which point Land turned to fight. They struggled furiously in the room and within minutes both went down on the floor, Land underneath the other man. Egan immediately got up and jumped on Land's chest, kicking him two or three times in the head as well.

Benjamin Chappell, the landlord, eventually separated them and ordered Egan to leave. Simpson quickly followed him. Land, who was unconscious, was put on the settle to recover. Within minutes it was realised that matters were more serious than had been thought. A local surgeon, Robert Keighley, who lived nearby in Harrison Street, was sent for but Land was already dead from 'extravasations of blood at the base of the brain' (leaking of blood from the blood vessel into the tissue which surrounds it).

The news of a death 'spread like wildfire' and a crowd, described as being of 'thousands', but more probably a few dozen, gathered outside the inn, which had to be closed to further business. Superintendent Martin of the borough police happened to be walking past and immediately took charge, offering a reward of ten shillings (50p) for the capture of Michael Egan.

On leaving the beer house, Egan and Simpson had gone to the *Wellington Inn,* but both were refused admittance. After this they went their separate ways, but Egan must have heard of Land's death or realised his predicament, because he went into a cottage and barricaded the door. The crowd soon traced him there and in a panic he rushed out, running towards an area known as Clark Green, to take refuge at the *White Hart Inn.* The crowd followed, but Egan was eventually 'collared' by William Simms, a local rope-maker. Constable Hudson soon arrived, handcuffed Egan and, closely followed by Simms who, no doubt, had his eye on the reward, was escorted down to Dewsbury Police Station.

The journey was not without incident. The Irish navvies, led by Patrick O'Neal (O'Nial), tried to rescue Egan. On Hick Lane, Hudson suddenly yelled out that the men were trying to trip him up. Simms got behind the constable to protect his back, when someone was heard to cry out 'That's the b***** that's seized Dummie' (Egan) and O'Neal rushed forwards, kicking Simms a number of times on his legs and thighs. Simms ran off to find Superintendent Martin and another constable who came to the rescue, but Simms 'never lost sight of him [Egan] until the constable took him into custody' at Dewsbury.

O'Neal later appeared at the police court charged with assault. Though Hudson had to admit he didn't see O'Neal actually do anything, he did say that the man was 'very obstinate and wouldn't behave himself, whatever was said to him'. That was enough for the judge, who said:

> *If people who are helping the police are to be interfered with in this way we shall never get on. We therefore send the prisoner to Wakefield House of Correction for two months.*

Simpson meanwhile was unaware of the hue and cry after him and wandered back to the Commercial Street beerhouse where PC English arrested him for being drunk and disorderly. It was only then that he realised he'd caught the man wanted for manslaughter and took him down to Dewsbury, where the two men appeared at the police court on

Wakefield Prison. The author

Monday morning. Both were remanded in custody, pending further investigations.

The inquest was heard on Tuesday, at the *White Hart Inn*, Batley before Mr G Jewison, coroner.

There was some confusion as to what actually happened. As more than one witness had to admit, no one was quite sober.

James Exley suggested that while Land was 'not exactly a fighting man' he had taken part in impromptu fights before and was known to be able to take care of himself.

Thomas Hepworth, a local butcher, agreed that Egan wanted to fight but Land refused, even going so far as to buy drinks for Egan as a sign of friendship. Land had said 'I'll go home' when he got up, trying to avoid the aggression, but Egan had stopped him until Mrs Chappell intervened. Hepworth agreed that Simpson and others were encouraging Egan to fight. Simpson had made signs of fighting to Egan and pointed at Land. Egan had obviously understood what Simpson wanted. No one was backing, or egging Land on to fight, and he tried his best to avoid it.

White Hart Inn, *Batley*. The author

David Castle, a painter, said he didn't know anyone else in the beer house but had seen what had happened. Land had tried to shake hands with Egan to calm things down, but Egan had seemed to want to go outside and fight, shaking his fists and pointing to the door. He also felt that Simpson had encouraged him. Later Castle had helped put Land on the settle where he 'sobbed once and died almost immediately'.

William Simpson denied having done anything wrong; saying in his defence that he had not struck any blows therefore could not possibly be guilty of manslaughter. The jury were equally certain that, since he had actively encouraged Egan in his actions, Simpson bore most of the blame. Though both were found guilty, the jury made a plea for mercy for Egan on the grounds of his disability.

Egan received three months' imprisonment, Simpson six months.

CHAPTER 6

An Innocent Child's Murder: Bingley 1837

I n April 1837, the coroner, Michael Stocks Jnr called an inquest to view the body of Harriet Bowman, of Bingley. There was more than enough evidence to commit her mother, Hannah Maude to York for trial for murder.

Sir G Lewin and Mr D Dundas acted for the prosecution, Mr Cottingman for the defence.

First of all Ann Pearson of Askham Bryan, York, explained that Hannah Maude (née Bowman) had once lived in the

St Helen's church, Stillingfleet. The author

,village, working as a dairymaid for John Jackson. In 1833, she had a baby girl, baptised in Stillingfleet church, though no one knew who the father was. Pearson took the baby to nurse and kept her for three and a half years. She was a very healthy child, but of 'a very obstinate temper'. The mother often came to see her but ill-treated her, having struck her with her fist on the back on at least one occasion when she was only nine months old. She'd said the child was hers and she would kill it if she liked. Later Hannah married and took the child away from the foster home.

Sarah Maude of Bingley, the prisoner's sister-in-law, spoke of her general ill-treatment of the child from the time she came home in January. Another sister had once taken the child from Hannah when she was beating it, but Hannah had said, 'If you take it away, I will kill it.' The child was quickly given back but when Hannah took Harriet inside, she knocked her down and 'poised it several times'. On another occasion Sarah Maude saw Harriet lying on the floor nearly naked. Hannah explained that the child would not say her prayers, so as punishment she was going to be left on the floor all night. It was a very cold night.

Two neighbours came forward to have their say. Elizabeth Smith said she had seen Harriet lying, quite naked, on the flags in front of the door on a cold, wet night. Hannah had come out of the house with a leather strap and flogged the child into the house. Ann Redrough informed the court that she had seen Hannah beat the little girl with a stick, causing several wounds. She had often seen the woman wipe blood off the floor. Mary Shaw had seen Hannah strike the child over the head with her fists. She heard her call the child ugly names and once had threatened to tear her liver out. Hannah had told her that 'if she had a mind to murder the child it was nothing to any one else'.

On 22 March, the Deputy Constable of Bingley, Edward Sutcliffe, finally went to see Harriet. George Dryden, surgeon, went on the same day and told Hannah she must have struck the child and ill-treated it. She immediately agreed that she had and 'would do so again'. Surprisingly, the little girl was left with the mother and not removed until the following morning, when she was taken to the workhouse. Hannah was taken into custody the same day, to be tried at Pontefract sessions for assaulting the child and had been in custody ever since.

On 12 April, little Harriet died. Mr Sharpe and Mr Dryden examined the body on the next day. They found a bruise on the right side of her forehead. The ears were sore as was the nose, with remnants of former ulcerations. One or two ulcers were found on the left shoulder and on the soles of the feet. Bruises were found on the right shoulder and elsewhere. Serum was found in the ventricle of the brain and extravasation of blood between the scalp and brain. On the right lobe of the lung was an abscess and tubercules as well as on the liver. The tubercules had been present for some time, possible as long as six months. The body was in a very unhealthy state. In the doctors' opinions, the child would have died of an abscess on the lungs chiefly but death was accelerated by external injuries. Such a disease might be brought on by cold and ill-treatment.

Mr Cottingham addressed the jury on behalf of the prisoner and called two witnesses to give her a good character.

The jury were so appalled by the evidence that they quickly found Hannah Maude guilty of manslaughter and she was sentenced to seven years' transportation. She was sent to the hulks to await a ship, staying there for three years before being transported on the ship known as *Surrey* to New South Wales.

CHAPTER 7

Wilful Murder: Boroughbridge
1844

C ountry markets are attended by all and sundry in the area. They're a good way of keeping in touch with people, as well as buying and selling a wide variety of goods.

Late one evening in October, 1844, William Inchbald of Low Dunsforth left the *Malt Shovel Inn* and set off home from Boroughbridge market. It quickly grew dark and by 6.30 it was beginning to rain. The lane was typical of its time – grassy verges with tall, thick hedges either side that created deep shade on either side of the path. Inchbald reached a very lonely section, near the junction of the rivers Swale and Ouse when he was shot between his shoulders. He turned round and

Malt Shovel Inn, *Boroughbridge*. The author

saw a man a few yards away, who fired a second time and hit him in the arm, before running away. Inchbald, who was a very strong man, survived and managed to stagger fifty yards before falling at the side of the road.

A few minutes later, John Topham drove his cart along the road, seeing what he thought was a man asleep at the side of the road. He passed him and drove to Inchbald's home, returning a short while later with Mrs Inchbald. Carefully lifting him into the cart, Inchbald was taken home and a doctor sent for, but to no avail. Inchbald died on the Monday morning.

It was not long before suspicion fell on William Kendrew. He had immediately fled the area and the *Leeds Mercury* described him as:

Aged 23 years old but looks older – 5' 10" or 11" high, rather square build, round shoulders, low forehead, light brown hair, short face, eyes rather sunken, large feet and shuffles in his walk.

Charles Inchbald of Aldborough, the murdered man's brother, offered a reward of £20 for Kendrew's capture.

The bridge at Boroughbridge. The author

Towards midnight on the night of the murder, a man named Barlow saw William Kendrew, with his older brother, John, crossing the bridge in Boroughbridge where John lived with their sister and her husband, a shoemaker named Joseph Scott. When the two men saw Barlow, they turned away and obviously didn't want to talk to him. By then the murder was common knowledge and Barlow ran for the police. The police gave chase and almost captured the Kendrew brothers but lost them in the darkness.

Later more information found its way to the police and on 7 October they went to Newcastle. As John Kendrew was a shoemaker (and deserter from the 12th Regiment of Foot) the police went to see Mr Binkey, a shoemaker, to see if anyone had applied to them for relief. It was he who sent them to the *Old Robin Hood Inn* where the shoemakers' society had its meetings and there they found William Kendrew among a number of army recruits. On being questioned, he gave his name as William Smith, from Leeds 'on the tramp'. He said the other man in the room was called John Palmer, but he'd only met him in the last week or so. When arrested by the police on a charge of shooting Inchbald at Boroughbridge, Kendrew immediately said it couldn't have been him as he wasn't there that week.

Nevertheless the two brothers found themselves in gaol, William charged with the shooting, John charged with 'feloniously harbouring and maintaining the said William Kendrew, well knowing him to have committed the said murder'.

At their trial in York, Mr Wilkins, Mr Overend, and Mr Price acted for the prosecution. The prisoners were undefended.

Mr Wilkins stated the case against the prisoners:

May it please your Lordship, gentlemen of the jury, I have little doubt that every one of you, upon entering that box, anticipating the duty that you had to discharge have prepared yourselves by every means for the arduous duty that you have to fulfil and that you are duly impressed with the importance of that duty, both as it affects the two prisoners now in the dock and as it affects the public interests. Gentlemen this is a case that will require as much consideration from you as any case that I ever had the honour of laying before a jury. The charge against the prisoner rests entirely upon circumstantial evidence. It will behove you well to keep an untiring eye upon that evidence as it proceeds because if you lose a link in the chain it may frustrate the object that you have in view, namely, the proper discharge of your duty. It does sometimes happen as has been said by one of our best commentators, that circumstantial evidence may be the most conclusive that can be brought before a jury. It is an easy matter for a wicked and ingenious person to concoct a story and to tell that story in the witness box with great firmness and apparent straightforwardness and thus impose upon a jury and destroy the happiness of his fellow men. But no man, be his ingenuity what it may, can fashion and frame a number of circumstances over which it is impossible that any human being can have control so as to bring with those circumstances overwhelming proof to the minds of the parties to whom he may address himself. Gentlemen, I will not anticipate what your verdict shall be but I will endeavour as far as in me lies, to keep my feelings in subjection to my reason and to lay the case before you calmly and dispassionately making no other observations than those which my duty seems to require and I hope that I shall not in any instance overstep the bounds of moderation and prudence knowing how fearful the consequences of this inquiry must be at any rate to one of the prisoners who stand in that dock.

The jury were given a series of plans to ensure that they were quite clear as to where all the events were happening.

Mr Wilkins then 'set the scene', describing Inchbald as a merchant who had retired from business and gone to live on his estate in Low Dunsforth. Most Saturdays he went to the Boroughbridge market. He was also of:

eccentric habits and was in the habit constantly of carrying a very large pocket book under his waistcoat and when he wanted any small document of constantly taking out this large pocket book and exhibiting it to any person who might be present. He was also in the habit – probably from some ostentatious motive – of taking out large quantities of gold and silver, when he had occasion to pay any account, however trifling it might be.

The surgeon, Roger Sedgewick, described the wounds, saying that there were 'more than fifty perforations'. He also told how Inchbald had informed him, just before his death, that he had heard the report of a gun and felt the shot in his shoulder.

John Buckle, of Great Ouseburn, was questioned about selling the shot, powder and caps to Kendrew. He looked intently at Kendrew in the dock and agreed that he was the man, but that the purchaser had looked 'six or seven years older than the prisoner'. He then went on to inform the court that he kept different kinds of shot in a box that had several compartments in it for the different sorts of shot. Sometimes shot from one size fell into the wrong compartment, but the same type of shot would be given from any shop in England if size 2 and 3 were asked for. It was quickly pointed out by the prosecution that on the Friday night when Kendrew purchased the ammunition, he asked for shots number 2 and 3 and he also asked for caps of different sizes 'for the nipples of my gun are one longer than the other'. Buckle seemed to feel it was his duty to give evidence, but didn't want to feel it was his evidence that would hang the man.

Kendrew's family seem to have less reluctance on this. His father, another William, his sister and her husband, Joseph Scott all gave evidence, which the prosecution used to good effect.

A week before the murder some young men had been on Boroughbridge Common shooting bats and they borrowed a gun from a person named Powell. One of them left the gun with the other and he took it home, leaving it in his master's stable. The lad had given the prisoner a lift as far as the stable; Kendrew had handled the gun and admired it. That gun had one nipple larger than the other and required two different sorts of caps. When the young man went to the stable again on the Sunday morning he found that the door, which he had locked on the previous night, had been opened and the gun was gone. At about two o'clock on the same day, Kendrew took some gun barrels out of his pocket to show to a man called Barlow. They examined them and noticed the peculiarity of the barrels. When asked where the stock of the gun was Kendrew said it was in his coat pocket. Later that week, on Wednesday night Kendrew went to his father's house, knocked at the door and asked to be admitted. At first his father seemed reluctant to do so, but he was told, 'If you don't let me in I will blow your brain out for I have a gun in my hand.'

On Saturday, Kendrew was at Boroughbridge, enquiring of a person named Fawcett whether he had seen anything of Inchbald that day. As far as the court knew he had no business with Mr Inchbald, there was no connexion between. At about two o'clock William Roberts saw Kendrew on the road to Dunsforth. Next a little girl named Mary Yates saw the prisoner, at about half past five, standing against George Thompson's white gate, near the middle of the road. At this time he had nothing in his hand. Just at this time a Mr Woodward came in sight and Kendrew immediately crossed the road and got into a goit in John Lumley's field and hid himself there until Mr Woodward had passed. It might seem odd for the court to accept a little girl's testimony, but when she had been telling the magistrates this tale at the initial trial, Kendrew was so surprised at the girl's statement that he blurted out:

Nay thou lies, I was as much as a hundred yards from thee when I went into the goit.

Mary Yates went on to tell how she saw that when Mr Woodward had gone by Kendrew had come out of the goit carrying a gun across his shoulder. He went along the inside of the field for a short distance towards Dunsforth and then got over two rails and got into the road.

Presumably he hid the gun behind a large manure heap, ready for later, since at a quarter past six, Kendrew, empty handed, was seen by a man named Smith Burrell walking slowly towards Inchbald, who was a few yards ahead going towards Dunsforth. Kendrew walked past Mr Inchbald, but when he'd got about fifty yards further he stopped. Burrell spoke to him but left him standing on the same spot. Later he looked behind and he saw that Kendrew had turned back and instead of being in front of Inchbald he was following him. Kendrew was wearing a cap and a fustian coat.

At 6.20 pm Ann Kirbyson saw Inchbald close to Mr Clay's house, on the same road. Shortly after this she met Kendrew midway between Thompson's White Gate and Aldborough. When Robert Horsman left Clay's cottage at 6.30 pm to go home by Sledbar Nook, he saw Kendrew walking quickly towards Dunsforth. Though Horsman spoke to him and tried to keep up with him it was obvious Kendrew did not want his company. A few yards further on he saw Mr Inchbald, who was also walking towards Dunsforth. As he reached home, he heard the sound of a gun that seemed to come from between Pick's farmhouse and Lumley's farm, which are near where the murder was committed.

Two further witnesses also swore to hearing the shots. Thomas Buck and William Robinson, who were both in nearby fields and heard two shots. Robinson also heard someone crying out 'Oh dear', three times, but does not seem to have bothered to investigate. Both men probably thought the shots were fired by poachers, who were often quite violent if their activities were disturbed, so decided discretion was the better part of valour.

It was believed by the prosecution that it was these cries of alarm by Inchbald that stopped Kendrew firing again and he then ran away across the fields towards Boroughbridge. It was about 7.30 when Mary Thompson saw him coming down the main street in Aldborough as if from York, and saw him go to 'Old Kendrew's house'. Around 8.00 pm John Umpleby, the village blacksmith, met William Kendrew and commented to him:

'Have you heard that Inchbald has been shot?'

Kendrew at first replied,

'Oh, be damned, it's all a lie.'

Umpleby insisted that it was true, and Kendrew eventually agreed that it may have been so. Surprisingly, in the prosecution's view, when Robert Horsman came up, Kendrew never mentioned the rumours or wanted to discuss the murder at all.

The two men walked along the street as far as Mr Lawson's garden door when they heard someone shouting out 'hello'. Kendrew immediately left Horsman and went to join the other person.

On the Sunday night after the murder, police officers went to Kendrew's father's house. There they made a search and in the thatch of the pigsty they found the gun with the barrels taken out of the stock. They also found hanging over the banisters a fustian coat, belonging to the prisoner, in which they found shot and powder. The shot was later compared with the shot taken from the wounds Inchbald received and proved to be 'of the same quality and character as those bought at Buckle's by the prisoner'.

Kendrew's sister stated that, on the Sunday night after the murder, she had a conversation with William, telling him that Bessy Tilburn had told her that Mr Inchbald had been shot by a man at Great Ouseburn with some No 3 shot bought at Boroughbridge. The prisoner asked her how they know what number the shot was and she replied that they had found some of it in his wounds. She also said they were in search of the man. William immediately asked, 'What could they make of the man if he had no shot upon him?' She had replied that it was impossible that Mr Inchbald could have done it himself. William had told her, 'Oh yes, he could have done it very well' and took great pains to show her how Inchbald could have done it himself.

Joseph Scott explained how William came to be at their house, saying that he had met William at *The Drover's Inn*, Boroughbridge on the night of the murder. Kendrew had complained that he had no bed to go to, which was a lie since he usually slept at his father's house. However, Scott told him, 'Thou can have half thy brother's bed who is lodging at our house.'

William had returned home with Scott but at about midnight they went out with some nets to fish and came back about half past one on Sunday morning, William remaining in bed on Sunday, whilst Scott went out. Sometime during those hours William and his brother, John, broke into the room of a lodger in the house and stole a pistol. Scott returned around seven at night. When he came in the house was in darkness, though William was sitting there with his sister.

Scott told him 'They are blaming thee for shooting Mr Inchbald.' William seemed surprised, but Scott continued, 'Yes and if thou art clear thou'll turn out and show thyself like a man and if thou isn't, thou shan't be long in my house.' Scott then threw the door open and stormed out.

William asked his sister to go and see which way her husband had gone and then go to an inn called the *Swales* and see if the rumours were true. When she returned and confirmed what her husband had said, she begged him to go and clear his name. William agreed that he would, but insisted that it would be in the morning, not that night. Despite his protestations of innocence, she replied, 'I'm afraid thou's guilty.'

It was that night William and his brother, John, left Boroughbridge.

The judge proceeded to sum up the case. He was very concerned that the prisoners did not have the benefit of a defence and pointed out that he:

> *wanted to do the prisoners justice but many of the facts were new to him on coming into court and as it was difficult for him to understand the depositions before him till he saw the plans in court this morning, it might easily happen that some points of considerable importance to the prisoners might have escaped his attention. If that infirmity applied to him, who was accustomed to try cases and to attend to points of evidence, he thought he might fairly without any improper reflection on the Jury suppose it would apply to them.*

Justice Coleridge then spent two hours going through all the details again. The jury took just fifteen minutes to find William Kendrew guilty, but his brother, John, not guilty of aiding and abetting him. John was removed from the dock and William asked if there was any reason why sentence should not be passed. He gave no reply, whereupon the judge donned the black cap, and:

Silence was proclaimed and he proceeded to pass the awful sentence of death upon the prisoner.

He remonstrated with the prisoner, telling him:

We cannot but judge that you premeditated the horrid deed hours I fear I may say days before you butchered your victim, that you dogged his steps and you effected your purpose as he was in perfect unconsciousness of danger returning to his home and to the wife of his bosom. You have done this with perfect deliberation. It is not now for me to dwell upon the enormity of your offence.

He went on to exhort Kendrew to think about his crime and to:

consider that your mortal life is short and that it will be closed in a painful and shameful way. I fear that the most wholesome and silent appeals are unknown to your heart. But in the short interval that remains to you on earth you will have the most faithful assistance in your spiritual concerns. I conjure you to lose no time if it be yet in time I conjure you from this moment abjure all thoughts of earth and seek an interest in the merits of the saviour. Open your heart to the prayers which will be offered on your behalf and try to secure your peace with God.

The judge seemed more affected at passing the sentence than Kendrew at receiving it. During the following week, whilst awaiting execution, Kendrew continued to insist he was innocent, even going so far as to send a letter to his friends to that effect. The Rev Thomas Sutton, York Castle chaplain, tried hard to get him to confess and his efforts were finally rewarded. On the Thursday before execution, Kendrew told Sutton that he had had no intention of robbing Inchbald; his motive was purely revenge. About a fortnight before the murder, Inchbald had threatened to have him transported for poaching. Kendrew deliberately lay in wait for the merchant, knowing that he would attend the local market and return late at night. He fired twice at Inchbald, then walked up to him and hit him with the butt of the gun.

On Saturday 28 December, William Kendrew was executed, having finally acknowledged the justness of his sentence and repented of his actions.

His brother John did not get off quite scot-free. He was brought before the court the following day on a charge of stealing a pistol, the property of Ann Glenton.

Ann was a widow who had begun trading as a milliner and dressmaker in order to support herself. She decided to go to Harrogate for a few weeks in order to 'improve herself in her calling' and let part of her house to Joseph Scott, Kendrew's brother-in-law. On Sunday 29 September, Kendrew broke into her room and stole the pistol, leaving that same night with his brother William and was not found until 7 October when they were both arrested in Newcastle. On being searched, a pawnbroker's ticket was found. The police went to the pawnbroker in Sunderland, recovered the pistol and the pawnbroker immediately identified Kendrew as the man who had pledged the item. The jury had no difficulty in finding him guilty.

The judge, in his sentencing, said that:

> he could not dismiss altogether from his mind the object for which the pistol was probably stolen ... and sentenced Kendrew to seven years' transportation.

CHAPTER 8

A Murderer Confessed: Bradford 1848

On 24 October 1848, young John Rushworth Broadley, an errand boy, set off for the warehouses in Hustler's Yard and saw something strange in the Bradford beck. Immediately, he sent for the police. Constable James Bolton soon arrived at the scene. In the swollen waters of the beck a male body was caught up against some posts. The officer dragged him out, noticing that his face was grimy and he had a scratch on his forehead. He was eventually identified as Robert Slater of Great Horton, a tailor, 'a remarkably quiet and inoffensive man and a peaceable neighbour'.

At first it was thought that he had drowned but the coroner, C Jewison, called an inquest as was required for a sudden and unexplained death. The jury included Edward Seed, carrier, Richard Spencer, registrar, Samuel Oddy, painter, John Tattersall, marble mason, Charles Taylor, plumber, Jonas Hill, joiner, John Bower, carpenter, John Binns, gent, Samuel West, manager, Edwin Trigg, grocer, William Shackleton, ironmonger and Edward Smith, shopkeeper and publican.

There was much discussion but little enlightenment until the police suddenly came into the courtroom and announced that a confession had been made. Joseph Foster from Great Horton had walked up to Constable Tilley's door that morning, confessed to the murder and surrendered himself.

He said that he was thirty years old and had been in the army but had been given a medical discharge about eighteen

MURDER AT BRADFORD, AND EXTRAORDINARY CONFESSION OF THE MURDERER.

The town of Bradford was thrown into a state

Headline, Leeds Mercury *1848*.
Author's collection

months ago, receiving a pension of sixpence a day because he was subject to fits. But the pension was only for two years and was about to end. Since leaving the army he had become a woolcomber, but this was not steady employment and he was frequently out of work, leading to equally frequent bouts of depression.

Mary ('Marguerite' according to *The Times*) Slater, the widow, confirmed her husband's identity, stating that he had been thirty-nine years old and a tailor by trade. On the Monday he died, he went off around noon with Joseph Bowles to go to Bradford for some cloth. That was the last time she saw him alive.

Joseph Bowles, shoemaker, confirmed the journey with Slater. In Bradford they went to Brook's shop and bought the cloth but split up for a short time after this – Slater going to buy some silk, while Bowles went to the *Nag's Head* to wait for him. At about four o'clock, Slater arrived and bought a quart (around two pints) of ale for them both and a noggin of rum (around a quarter of a pint). After this it was Bowles' turn to go shopping, buying some leather for shoemaking, while Slater went on to Abraham Priestley's inn a little further up the road. Bowles joined him there and they had another glass of ale. The two men left their purchases at Brook's shop and went on to Slater's father-in-law's house in Silsbridge Lane, where they stayed until six o'clock, then visiting another neighbour. When they left it was dark and raining, so they went to another beer shop, the *Navigation Inn* and stayed there until eleven at night, when they were turned out. He admitted they'd had 'a good few pints of ale' but it had all been good-natured. Joseph Foster was there, along with others, and they'd all enjoyed a bit of a song and been merry together.

Except that at one time, Robert Slater had left the room and returned with his face covered in mud, but refused to say what had happened.

Joseph Foster and his friends left first. Slater, Bowles and another friend, Joseph Gomersall, all left together and went down to the *Royal Hotel* on Silsbridge Lane. Bowles had a pint of ale, but Slater only had water as he said he 'felt sickly'. An hour or so later, just after midnight, Slater and Bowles left together, both quite drunk. They walked past Gomersall's house, but he had already told them not to bother calling and disturbing his wife. Bowles stopped to relieve himself and then fell down in a drunken stupor. A little later he woke up and thought he heard Slater call out, but though he followed the sound, Bowles could not see his friend so decided to return home. He knocked on Slater's front door to see if he had got home, but he was not there, Mary Slater frostily informing Bowles that it was one o'clock in the morning.

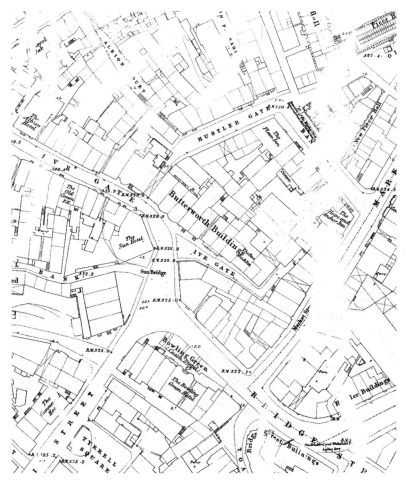

Map of Sun Bridge, Bradford. Ordnance Survey

William Brooksbank was a silversmith of Market Street, Bradford. His house backed on to the Bradford beck, which was swollen with recent rain. On the Monday night he had sat up late, and around 2 am he thought he heard a noise, as of some people talking in the yard, then it faded until eventually he heard a cry as of someone crying for help. And continued:

Immediately after I heard footsteps as of someone running away. The sound of the crying died away rapidly.

Then Constable Tilley told the tale of how the prisoner had arrived at his house that morning, asking him to go with him to Bradford. Once they were outside the house, Foster had told him, 'I am the person who threw the man over the Sun Bridge on Tuesday morning between one and two o'clock.'

When asked why, Foster had replied:

I am destitute of a home; my father does not behave well to me; I am tired of my life and I want to have an end of it.

On the constable's remark that he would have done something other than take a man's life, Foster said:

I do not want to be transported, I want to be hung; some men's lives are a pleasure to them, but I am miserable.

He confirmed Bowles statements that they had been in the same pub, drunk happily together and he had no quarrel with Slater, nor had he wanted to rob him. There was no struggle. He just threw the man over the bridge. He had not even followed him, it was just chance that they both happened to be in the same place. He continued to the officer:

I thought you were a decent sort of a chap, and I would give you the job.

The coroner cautioned Foster and asked if he wanted to make any statement in his defence. Foster continued:

I have intended for some time to do something to bring myself to the gallows and if a smaller offence would have done so, I should have been glad to have committed it … If I had studied about it I should not have done it. I determined to put an end to my own life.

The coroner's jury brought in a verdict of wilful murder against Foster and he was taken to York Castle for trial.

At the assizes, the same evidence was heard, prompting the judge to recall Constable Tilley and ask him if Foster usually 'knew what he was about?' Tilley replied that he did.

Next, the surgeon, Joseph Poppleton, was called. When he stated categorically that the deceased had died from drowning, the judge asked him if he had performed a post-mortem examination and opened the body. No, the surgeon had not done so, he knew a drowned man when he saw one. But he also confirmed that a drunken man could not fall into the beck, the parapet of the Sun Bridge was so high. The judge was still not impressed.

It is a very superficial way of concluding that a man is drowned because he is found in the water (The Times).

He then summed up for the jury, directing them to consider whether the man drowned or not, given that there was no proper post-mortem, but also to consider the state of mind of the prisoner.

If he intended to commit this offence in order to be hanged, it would be thought by most people that he would have gone at once and confessed it (The Times).

Perhaps he had changed his mind, but this case was so far outside normal experience that it could not be judged by ordinary principles. Did the prisoner intend to drown the man? If so, he was guilty as charged. If the jury had any doubt, they must acquit the prisoner.

After an hour's deliberation, the jury found Foster not guilty.

But this was not the end of the matter. The prosecution couldn't quite believe that the jury had not believed Foster's statement. The prisoner too seemed quite upset, saying that he had been quite prepared to be hanged.

The governor of York Castle, Mr Shepherd, then stated that he felt the prisoner was quite insane because he had had a number of fits whilst in gaol and had been quite 'outrageous' after them.

The judge decided not to discharge Foster but suggested that there were cases where the parish could take charge of pauper lunatics, but it was pointed out that Foster had not yet become chargeable as a pauper. Finally, it was agreed that some sort of arrangement would be made for Foster to be confined in an asylum and his parish made to pay for it.

All quotes are from the *Leeds Mercury*, unless stated otherwise.

CHAPTER 9

The Big Bank Robbery: Brighouse 1837

The Huddersfield Banking Company was one of the first joint stock banks to be opened in Yorkshire. In January 1828 it celebrated opening its first permanent offices with a dinner at the old *George Inn*, Huddersfield, attended by some of the most important men in the district. The bank expanded rapidly, opening branches in Brighouse, Dewsbury, Holmfirth, Batley and Heckmondwike. In 1897 it merged with the equally prestigious Midland Bank, which in turn has become the HSBC.

In Christmas 1836 plans were being laid. John Thornton, a thirty-year-old weaver, told his friend, James Lister, from Shelf,

Old George Inn, *Huddersfield*. The author

near Bradford, that he and some pals were intending to rob 'some place in Brighouse'. In April, he met up in Halifax with George Atkinson, a young man of twenty-two. Lister was asked if he would definitely join the conspirators and he agreed. He was immediately taken to a public house between Hipperholme and Brighouse where he met the others – John Hayley, a twenty-two-year-old blacksmith from Halifax, and Joseph Dodson (or Dodgson) a thirty-one-year-old waterman from Huddersfield as well as his friend, Thornton. Another man was present, but Lister did not know him, nor was he introduced.

The rest of the gang then went off together, whilst Lister kept lookout.

On the night of 21 April 1837 the bank's clerk, George Hall, closed the Brighouse branch of the Huddersfield Banking Company. The Brighouse branch had only just opened in 1837 and bank business was conducted in a small room in his house. The room was connected by a short passage to the rest of the building.

George carefully counted out £267 in gold, almost £29 in silver, £595 in Bank of England notes, £200 in £10 notes and £745 in £1 notes of the Huddersfield Banking Company, together with £196 notes from other small banks. There were also eight drafts of the Huddersfield Banking Company on Smith, Payne & Co, in London, which together with other bills amounted to almost £252. All this was put in a tin box, fastening it with a padlock and putting it into an iron safe. He then barred and locked the door into the street, though the passage door was open. Hall retired to bed.

Around four in the morning two boys roused the bank clerk from sleep. When he got down stairs he found that a panel had been cut out of the door into the street and the door was open. The iron safe was found discarded one hundred and fifty yards away. All the money was gone.

Thornton and his gang got away with almost £2,000 but they refused to pay Lister more than a couple of guineas for his trouble, then went their way with their ill-gotten gains. Three of the stolen bills were later found in a nearby stable, discarded probably because the gang felt it would not be possible to cash them.

It was much later, in August 1837, that Lister fell foul of the law. According to some reports, he had been at Norland fair and run out of money. Aggrieved at having received such a small sum for his part in the robbery he accosted his friends, demanding more money as his share of the robbery. Not surprisingly this was overheard and information immediately given to the Huddersfield police. The police denied this, insisting that they already had their sights on Lister and arrested him because of other information received.

However they came by the information, Lister was soon in custody and immediately turned Queen's Evidence, giving sufficient details to ensure the arrest of Joseph Dodson and John Thornton of Moldgreen near Huddersfield, with several others who had been concerned in various robberies over the previous few months. When Constable Christopher Cheesbrough went to Thornton's house he found two dark lanterns, proof as far as the police were concerned that Thornton was up to no good.

Lister also gave evidence against George Atkinson of Leeds and John Hayley of Halifax. Haley and Atkinson were arrested in Salford, where a sharp-eyed officer, PC Diggles, spotted them with a man named Gray as they were going into a public house near the Liverpool and Manchester railway station. After their arrest, Haley was found to have thirty-nine sovereigns on him, which he insisted he had received in the way of business.

Whilst in prison, Richard Sharpe, a special constable, overheard Dodson and Thornton muttering together about their situation. Thornton had stated that he was sure if they had only given Lister two or three sovereigns more, he would not have said anything about them. Dodson replied, 'He'll get us served out, Jack.' Further discussion included the need for a good counsellor, and the difficulty of turning the notes into sovereigns, which Thornton felt would not be too difficult as 'some of their folk would be up in time in the morning'.

The four men appeared before Huddersfield magistrates in August 1837, where they were committed to York Assizes.

On 3 March 1838 they appeared at the Crown Court before Mr Justice Coleridge. Sergeant Atcherley, Mr Baines and Mr

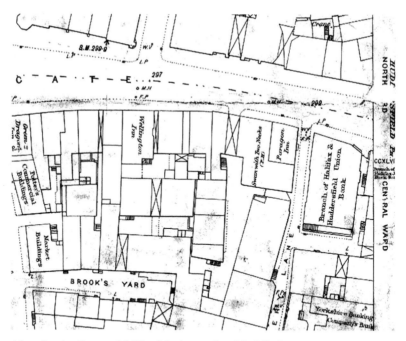

Map showing Swan with Two Necks *on site of* Saddle Inn. Ordnance Survey

Adolphus prosecuted; Mr Dundas and Mr Bliss defended the prisoners.

The defence was largely based around discrediting the prosecution witness, James Lister, who was also well known to the police, having been charged with many other robberies. All the defendants denied knowing each other, Haley insisting that he had not even been in Brighouse for over four years. However, James Armitage, whose father ran the *Saddle Inn* at Huddersfield (later the *Swan with Two Necks*) stated that he saw Atkinson and another man in there on the day after the robbery, discussing how to get rid of the 'soft goods' – presumably the stolen notes - after which, getting rid of the 'hard goods' – ie the gold and silver - would be easy.

Despite Mr Dundas' passionate plea on behalf of the prisoners, the jury decided they were all guilty, and all four were sentenced to death. Subsequently, this was commuted to transportation for life.

John Thornton was baptised in Kirkheaton. He was the only one of the men who was married, though he was no saint, being convicted twice for bastardy and once for vagrancy. He did, though, have one legitimate child too. John Haley was born in Halifax and had also been in trouble with the law a number of times previously. Joseph Dodgson came from Huddersfield and had previous convictions for bastardy and vagrancy. George Atkinson seems to have come from Leeds and was also well known to the law.

They were all transferred to the hulk ship, *Justitia*, moored at Woolwich and from there to the ship *Coromandel*, which sailed to Van Dieman's Land (now Tasmania), in June 1838, arriving there in October, after a four months' voyage.

CHAPTER 10

Strange Death of a Sister-in-Law: Brighouse
1877

Bessey, the eldest daughter of George and Maria Kershaw, was a bit of a disappointment. Not that she was ever described on any of the censuses as an 'imbecile', and in fact, she was even able to work a little as a card seller. But it has to be said that she was more than a bit slow.

However, the family coped with her and she thrived in the security of her parents' home. The problem began when her father died in 1872, followed at the beginning of 1876 by the death of her mother. Someone else in the family had to be responsible for her and that responsibility fell to her younger brother, James and his wife, Maria.

She went to live with them in a healthy state, despite being subject to epileptic fits. Within a year she was dead.

On 8 January 1877 police inspector Eli Haigh went to the Kershaw's house, following notification of the death of Elizabeth. Both her eyes were black and bloody, there was a deep gash on the back of the head and she had a running abscess on her leg. Haigh was so horrified by the state of the woman's body that he ordered her to be undressed. It was then he saw the extent of the bruising – the whole of the body was covered in bruises, ranging from newly created purple to fading yellow. He asked Maria Kershaw how the injuries had

Headline Leeds Mercury *1877.*
Author's collection

INHUMAN TREATMENT OF AN IMBECILE AT BRIGHOUSE.

MARIA KERSHAW (25), married, who was found Guilty (with a recommendation to mercy) of the manslaughter of Elizabeth Kershaw, at Brighouse, on the 7th January last, was brought up to receive sentence.—His LORDSHIP (addressing the prisoner) said— It is perfectly impossible to imagine anything more

Albion Inn, *Brighouse, now a takeaway.* The author

occurred but she denied all knowledge of them. She thought perhaps it was because Elizabeth had fallen down the cellar steps the previous day and spilt paraffin, but 'she always wore a handkerchief' so Maria had never noticed the head wound, nor the blood.

Inspector Haigh looked carefully at the cellar steps but could find no sign of any blood. Next he examined the dress Elizabeth had been wearing, but there was no sign or smell of any paraffin. The only witness to these falls had been Maria's husband.

The following day, an inquest was opened by coroner Mr Barstow, at the *Albion Inn*, Brighouse, on the body of Elizabeth Kershaw. The jury consisted of Edward Heaton, foreman; Thomas Hill, Matthew Wadsworth, Joseph Bottomley, Joseph Schofield, Charles Heaton, Alfred Brook, Secker Blackburn, Samuel Turner, Alfred Mann, Jonathan Marsden and John Hodgson.

The local doctor, George Hoyle, explained that he had examined the body and found it covered in bruises and in a very emaciated condition. Death, he believed, was caused by shock from the battering she had received. Not even a large number of falls, he thought, could have caused such extensive bruising. William Charteris, the surgeon called in to assist at the post-mortem, agreed wholeheartedly with his colleague – the bruising, he was sure, was not the result of epileptic fits but of regular beating.

James Kershaw confirmed that after the death of both their parents, he had taken her in to save her from being sent to the workhouse – no one else in the family would have her. She had been subject to fits since she was three years old and was not able to have any real employment but could do such jobs as washing up under supervision. She needed to be watched constantly, like a small child. He said she had been ill for the past few days, and on Friday he had noticed her eyes were swollen and 'she could scarcely see'. On Friday morning he noticed that her eyes, which had been black, had turned red and begun to swell. He put her injuries down to her epilepsy. In her younger days she had been run over by a carriage, and twice been burnt because of the fits. In reply to the doctor's accusation of her being malnourished, he stated that she was given the same food as the rest of the family, except for meat, which she was unable to chew.

Hannah Allen, who was present when Elizabeth died, said she had seen her earlier on that day and in 'a sad condition'. She told the coroner about the events of the day, describing the blood, which seemed to be 'tainted with matter' which was streaming from both eyes. She asked Maria what had happened and Maria replied that she thought it was an infection. Both the Kershaws said they had sent for a doctor but none had come before Elizabeth died.

The two women, together with another neighbour, Eliza Allen, began to lay out the body. It was then that the extent of the bruising on her starved body was seen. Maria insisted initially that they had all been caused by falling whilst in a fit, then said that Elizabeth had fallen down the stairs. When Hannah questioned her about the bruises on Elizabeth's arms, Maria replied:

Don't say anything, will you, Hannah? If the police get hold of it there is no telling what they will make of it.

Though neither of the women had actually seen Maria ill-treat her sister-in-law, both felt the woman was not given enough to eat, and Eliza, who did washing for Maria, said she had never been asked to wash any clothing for the deceased.

Another neighbour, Ann Shaw, told how she had taken Maria to task about Elizabeth's black eyes and received a very offensive reply for her troubles. Her little girl, Margaret, used to visit the Kershaws to help with their little girl, Lillie, but one day in December Margaret had returned home very upset because, she said, she had seen Maria striking Elizabeth a number of times across the face simply because she had put some bowls in the wrong place.

The foreman of the jury commented that 'there had been some reluctance on the part of some of the witnesses to give evidence' which was not really surprising since they were all friends and neighbours of the family. The coroner pointed out that if someone other than the deceased herself had caused the bruises, there was no evidence to point to anyone except Maria Kershaw. Why Maria's husband, James, was not accused of the injuries is unknown. After five hours of sifting evidence, the coroner's jury brought in a verdict of manslaughter against Maria Kershaw, who was committed to the magistrates' court.

On 24 January Maria Kershaw appeared at the West Riding Courthouse in Halifax, before magistrate Captain Rothwell, charged with the manslaughter of her sister-in-law. Her neighbour, Harriett Schofield, told the court of seeing Maria striking her sister-in-law and pulling her around by the hair. Ann Shaw not only spoke of the numerous times she had seen the poor woman with black eyes but also said she had seen Maria knock Elizabeth against the hot bars of the fire grate, causing an open wound. Even the couple's babysitter, Emily Allen, who was only twelve, said she had been in the house when Elizabeth had been sent to fetch coal for the fire and seen Maria hit Elizabeth with a piece of wood when she dropped the coal scuttle. Later, when Elizabeth brought small bits of coal rather than larger lumps, Maria attacked her again with the wooden stick. The magistrates sent Maria to the assizes.

In March, she appeared before Justice Lopes in Leeds. The evidence was reiterated, with the defence making much of Elizabeth's fits. Dr Hoyle agreed that it was possible some of the bruises, and the head wound, could have been caused by falling during an epileptic fit but still felt that the extent of the bruising, and the fact that they had been inflicted over a considerable period of time, suggested that they were deliberately inflicted by someone. His colleague, Charteris, agreed. The wounds must have bled considerably and wrapping them in a handkerchief would not have concealed all the blood. If Elizabeth had sustained the wounds in falling down the steps, it would have been impossible for her to walk upstairs to her bedroom, therefore someone else had inflicted the wounds or the Kershaws must have been aware of the injuries and should have called in medical assistance earlier.

Mr Gane suggested to the jury that 'although it was clear that the deceased had died from certain wounds, yet there was no evidence to connect the prisoner with having inflicted them'. He produced two character witnesses – Samuel Kershaw who was the deceased's brother, who stated that Maria was generally a kind woman; and J W Willans, who had employed Maria and always found her to be of 'good character and kind in demeanour'.

The jury retired to consider their verdict, eventually deciding that Maria was guilty but recommending mercy in view of her previous good character.

The following day Maria was brought up for sentencing. Judge Lopes informed her that, once Elizabeth came to live with her, 'it was your duty to have protected her but she gradually became thin and her appearance gave evidence of cruel treatment'. He went on:

... there may be those who think that poor afflicted creatures like Elizabeth Kershaw, to whom is denied the full power of reason, may be maltreated with impunity ... the laws of England are made for all and especially to protect the weak from the strong. The sanctity of human life must be defended ...

Despite the recommendation for mercy, Maria was sentenced to ten years in prison.

No action seems to have been taken against Maria's husband who, presumably, should have known how his sister was being treated in his own home. He and their daughter, Lillie, eventually went to live with another brother, Samson and his family in Southowram.

Elizabeth was buried in a family grave in Lightcliffe cemetery.

Lightcliffe Church Tower. The author

CHAPTER 11

By Persons Unknown at Ledsham:
Castleford
1869

n Wednesday 22 September 1869 a coroner's inquest was held at the *Pointers' Inn*, South Milford to view the body of Richard Kellett of Ledsham, near Castleford.

Thomas Kellett, a farm bailiff of Middleton, identified the body as his brother, Richard, but said he had not seen him for the past two years.

Thomas Scott, the surgeon from Sherburn had known Richard Kellett for at least twenty years. When he had first seen the body, there seemed to be only a small graze on his forehead and a small wound near it. He had conducted the post-mortem, finding a discolouration of the skin above the left ear, but no swelling. It was only when he took off the scalp that he found a large quantity of blood covering the area between the periosteum (the membrane or tissue covering a bone) and the scalp. The left temple had a two-inch fracture. Scott gave his opinion that the blood had come from the left meningeal artery and this would have been sufficient to cause death. One blow behind and above the left ear would be sufficient to produce both the rupture and the lacerations. Such a wound could have been caused by a blow from a blunt instrument or by a bad fall.

The surgeon told the court that, after the blow, the deceased would not have been able to walk very far, if at all.

Christopher Scholes, hatmaker, of Castleford, described how he found the body, explaining that he had been walking from Ledsham towards Sherburn with his family, crossing the fields along a footpath:

When we got about one hundred and fifty yards from this house and about twenty yards from the stile I found the deceased laid with his left leg straight out and his right leg doubled up under it. His head and shoulders were on the bank under the hedge. He was lying on his back; a felt hat was laid against his right leg. His left hand was straight out and his right hand was under his thigh. His coat was open and his waistcoat was fastened. He had apparently vomited on his waistcoat shirt and trousers. His mouth was covered with froth and there was a little dried blood about his nostrils. (Taylor notebooks)

Scholes called for help from a farm labourer he saw in the next field and then went on to Sherburn to inform Mr Parkin, inspector of police. Scholes noticed particularly that the turnips which grew close up to the footpath weren't trampled down, as if the deed had been done quickly, with little scuffling.

Whilst Scholes went to Sherburn, the farm labourer went for Fairburn's police constable, John Dyson. Dyson told the coroner that he went to the footpath and saw the body lying in a sitting position with its back against the bank of the hedge. He had the body removed to the granary of the farm and examined the pockets. Robbery was obviously not a motive since the constable found a purse with £7 10 shillings (£7.50) in gold, and further change in the trouser and smock pockets as well as a silver watch.

Farmer Francis Morritt of Ledsham came forward to say that the deceased worked on his farm, starting about three months earlier. He appeared to be on good terms with the other workers, who included Thomas Conlon, James Cryan and Michael Gowan (McGovan). His son, Thomas, told how on the Tuesday before the murder he'd seen Thomas Conlon in the stackyard with Kellett. Conlon had seemed angry and was shouting that he would fight Kellett if only he would come down the ladder. Morritt immediately sent Conlon off to work in one of the fields, but never saw any sign of unpleasantness between the two men afterwards. On the night of the murder, he saw Conlon and Gowan at about 8 pm in the fold leading to the granary where they slept . They had a key to the granary and could go in and out as they pleased.

Then Robert Wilson of Ledsham, who worked at Elvidge's farm, said that he had known Kellett for the last three or four months. The previous Monday they had both gone to the Harvest Thanksgiving at Ledsham church, though Wilson did not see the deceased until later. They left at about five o'clock, going on to Samuel Barrett's public house. Esau Blacker, John Broadbent and others came in afterwards. Thomas Conlon, the third man, was at the pub door when Wilson and Kellett were

Ledsham Church. The author

leaving with Blacker and Broadbent. Kellett invited Conlon to 'Come and have a walk with me' but Conlon refused and the group set off to accompany a friend, John Leconby, part of the way on his journey to Wetherby. When they got to the *Boot & Shoe Inn* they went in for a last drink together and then went on towards Micklefield Station. Broadbent, Blacker, Wilson and Kellett saw their friend off and then returned to the *Boot & Shoe Inn*, leaving there about nine at night. About two hundred and fifty yards from the *Boot & Shoe* they met a man in a white smock, 'a stiff man and not tall'. Kellett stopped and talked to him, commenting on the fine, moonlit night, and then the two friends turned to walk on together. As they did so, the man lashed out at Wilson, striking him on his head with a stick and then attacking Kellett, who ran back to the *Boot & Shoe*. Wilson tried to get up but was knocked down again, then the man ran after Kellett, followed by two others. As Wilson again tried to get up, another man appeared and knocked him down again, kicking him as well. Wilson cried out, 'Oh, give over you are making my head bleed'. He managed to escape and hid in the hedge bottom for a while before going home. Wilson stated that the first man they had spoken to was Irish. Blacker and Broadbent, who were some distance behind the others, ran away as soon as the fracas started.

John Broadbent and Esau Blacker confirmed Wilson's version of the events of the evening, saying that the men who attacked them all spoke with Irish accents.

Ann Barratt wife of Samuel John Barratt of Ledsham, carpenter and landlord of the *Chequers Inn*, said she had seen Kellett go out of her house with John Leckonby between six and seven o'clock on Monday night. There were three Irishmen men who came into the kitchen a few minutes before Kellett left. She did not notice them leave, but they had gone by half past seven. All the men appeared to be on friendly terms. However, the previous Saturday night Kellett was at her house when Thomas Conlon came in with a stranger. Conlon nudged the stranger's elbow and said, 'That's the man,' indicating towards Kellett. The stranger had a stick with him. Later she saw all three together and they appeared to be on good terms.

Samuel John Barratt confirmed his wife's testimony, saying that the deceased frequently went to the pub in the evening but never stayed long. On Saturday 18 September Kellet and Conlon had been at his house. Three other Irishmen were also there and they appeared to be friendly – Kellett had paid for beer for the whole party. At about ten o'clock, Kellett left with two other men, Bleasby and Gibson, going out of the front door. Almost immediately, Conlon went out through the back door and one of the Irish men, a stranger, went out of the front door. The stranger had a thickish stick. He and Conlon came in again together about ten minutes later. On the following Monday evening, Barratt saw Conlon, with James Cryan and Michael Gowan together. Cryan appeared to be drunk. Just after Kellett left, Conlon and Gowan also left, Cryan following a short while later.

On the Monday evening, Henry Brown, a corn miller's apprentice, had been driving a cart from Kippax to South Milford. Near the Ledsham stile he saw four Irishmen on the road. After leaving his load at the *Pointer Inn*, he returned by the same route and saw the same men speaking a language he did not understand. 'They all appeared to be of middle size and stiffly built,' he said. His boss, John Archer of Sherburn, confirmed the lad's tale.

As a consequence of the statements made to him, Inspector Thomas Parkin arrested the three Irishmen – Thomas Conlon, James Cryan, and Michael Gowan (aka McGovan). He charged them with the wilful murder of Richard Kellett, Conlon replied, 'The Lord in Heaven knows I'm innocent.' Gowan said, 'I am innocent of the job' and Cryan also said, 'I am innocent'. They were taken to the police station in Sherburn but it was not until the following day that the Inspector noticed a stain on Conlon's trousers

Thomas Scattergood, surgeon. University of Leeds

just below the knee of the right leg. The stain looked like blood and seemed as if he'd tried to wash it out. Conlon confirmed that he had been wearing the same trousers on the Monday of the murder, but when Parkin pointed the stain out to Conlon, the prisoner replied, 'If it is blood I got it in the cells while kneeling down to say my prayers.'

Parkin promptly inspected the floor of the cell, which was quite clean with no traces of any blood. The trousers were taken to Inspector William Murray of Leeds who also felt that the stains were of blood and that an attempt had been made to wash them. He took the trousers to Thomas Scattergood, a surgeon and lecturer in medical jurisprudence at the Leeds School of Medicine. Scattergood agreed with the two policemen – they were bloodstains and they had been washed. Although it could not be confirmed, Scattergood thought that the appearance was that of human blood.

Despite all the evidence put before them, the jury decided that it was not enough and brought in a verdict of 'wilful murder against person or persons unknown'. No further action was taken against the suspected Irishmen.

CHAPTER 12

A Death at Dawgreen: Dewsbury 1871

In the 1840s, in common with many other Irish, William Armstrong and his wife, Margaret, brought their family, nine-year-old Anna and six-year-old Patrick, across the sea to Dawgreen near Dewsbury. With them were Margaret's brother, Patrick Reynolds and his wife Catherine. Finding work in the local mills, the family thrived, with the addition of Fanny in 1850, Catherine in

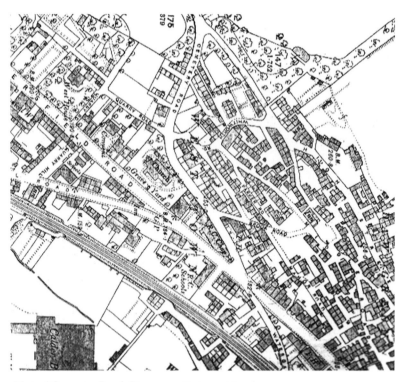

Map of Cemetery Road, Dawgreen. Ordnance Survey

1855, Margaret in 1859, Mary in 1860 and William in 1862. As the family grew up, they too went into the mills. But shortly after young William was born, his father died. Margaret took lodgings with Fanny Conlon, moving in with her children, Margaret and William.

During the same years, the Taylor family had grown up in Earlsheaton where their father, Joseph, had been a cloth finisher. Son Joseph also became a cloth finisher and moved to live in Cemetery Road, Dawgreen with his wife, Sarah. At some point, Joseph senior moved to Whitworth Road in Dawgreen. By 1871 he too was a widower.

Margaret Armstrong and Joseph Taylor began an association that was to end in death.

On Monday 11 September 1871 the Mayor of Dewsbury, Mr Ridgway, accompanied the magistrate's clerk to a cottage in Dawgreen, Dewsbury. There they intended to interview Joseph Taylor who had been reported as being seriously injured and at the point of death. They were too late. Though still alive, Taylor never regained consciousness and died on Tuesday.

On Wednesday, Thomas Taylor, the coroner, held an inquest at the *Horse and Jockey Inn* at Dawgreen. It was alleged that Margaret Armstrong, who was described as 'a paramour of his with whom he lived', had inflicted the injuries. According to Margaret, Joseph had hit his head on the kerbstone on Saturday night. She made little of the fact that she had pushed him out of the house at that time.

The jury was sworn in and Albert Winch chosen as foreman. Joseph Taylor junior, was called to identify the body. He confirmed that the deceased man was his father, Joseph, who was sixty-one years old, a widower and blanket weaver, though recently he had become a pea hawker. Taylor senior had been a 'strong and active man' though he enjoyed his beer rather too much.

Young Joseph said he had heard his father 'cry peas' around six on Saturday evening but didn't actually see him. On Sunday afternoon he had called at his father's house 'for a pipe' but found him in bed and unconscious. He noticed a bruise on the man's forehead, but failed to rouse his father, shaking him and calling out to ask how he'd got the bruise. Margaret Armstrong had been there too and she said, though she hadn't been in the house when it happened, the man must have fallen and hit his head against a large earthenware pot about two feet high, used for storing the dried peas. A large pan of cooked peas was on the stove, ready for Taylor senior to go out to sell. Taylor junior had seen his father in just such a state many times before, so simply collected his pipe and left, thinking there was nothing seriously wrong.

However, when he returned on Monday evening, his father was lying in just the same state, but by now froth was bubbling from his nose and mouth. He asked Margaret if she had called a doctor and she said both Dr Connon and Mr Smithson had been, but neither had prescribed any treatment, so Joseph went to fetch Mr Wooler, a local GP who lived near Taylor junior in Cemetery Road, who suggested weak brandy and water, but to no avail. Joseph stayed with his father through the night until, around eleven o'clock on Tuesday morning, the old man died.

He told the court that his father and Armstrong had been living together for about four years and were often drunk. He'd lived with them previously in Earlsheaton and had often seen them in that state.

Emma Field, from Dewsbury Moor, next told the coroner how she had been in Whitworth Road on Saturday evening, at about a quarter to six. She'd walked through the ginnel near the Taylor house, heard sounds of an argument so went to see what was happening. She saw Margaret Armstrong there, holding Taylor by the right shoulder with her left hand and thumping him in the stomach with her right fist. Armstrong then grabbed Taylor with both hands and threw him out of the house. He landed hard on the roadway, banging his head on the pavement. However, he got up, rubbed his hands on the back of his head and began shouting abusive foul language at her. It seemed as if he was going to go back into the house, but Armstrong, who also appeared to be the worse for drink, quickly shut the door on him, so he picked up his cap and walked up Whitworth Road, still shouting abuse. He made no attempt to hit Armstrong, but went off up the road.

Their neighbour, Nancy Ambler, a dressmaker and wife of a stonemason who had gone to Africa, also saw Taylor on Saturday, once with his can of peas but later too when he 'had bad beer, but she had seen him worse'.

At around seven o'clock she heard shouting and on going out found that Armstrong was asking him for money to pay the rent but he simply shouted abuse and said he would pay the rent himself, presumably not trusting her to use any money for rent rather than drink. Armstrong then grabbed the man, demanding money, pulling him towards her by his waistcoat then pushing him away so hard he fell, banging his head on the pavement so hard Nancy heard the thud. He could not get up and lay there. Nancy's youngest son, William, went to see if he could help, shouting, 'Mother, come and help us in with him.' Armstrong refused to help, saying, 'The b*****'s dead. I've a box for him inside.' When William said there was a cart coming, her reply was simply, 'Let the b***** cart run over the b*****.' The driver helped Nancy and her son get Taylor inside, helped eventually by Armstrong, along with 'several children', who may have been Armstrong's youngest children – Margaret, thirteen and William, nine. Nancy saw no sign of Emma Field, and was adamant that the couple had been on the pavement, not the doorstep. She agreed that there had been an earlier argument, but had not bothered to go out to that one. She heard nothing of any pots being broken.

Nancy stated that the couple had been quarrelling day and night, but this was a regular thing with the pair, though Taylor was generally noisier than Armstrong. When she next saw Taylor, around ten o'clock on Monday morning, he was in bed and 'insensible'. Her daughter, Mary, told how she had seen Taylor in Middle Road early on Saturday afternoon and round about the district during the day. The arguments with Armstrong had started around four o'clock and continued all afternoon. Around seven that evening, she saw Taylor outside his house and saw Armstrong 'click' (get hold of) Taylor and ask him for some money. He refused and said he'd pay the rent himself, at which point she threw him backwards. Mary was certain that he didn't strike her, but that neither did

Armstrong actually strike the man, she had hold of him and threw or pushed him backwards, which was when he hit his head on the ground. Later, Mary recalled that Armstrong had hired some boys to beat up Joseph Taylor, bruising his face. No one else seems to have stated this.

The surgeon, William Connon, was called to the house on Monday morning around half past eleven. Taylor was in bed but unconscious and could not be roused. He asked Armstrong about the bruise on the man's head and she again said it was caused by falling against an earthenware bowl when he was drunk. The doctor was told that he had a bruise on the back of his head as well, so called again around four o'clock. Taylor was still unconscious. On examination, he found the bruise which was not much bigger than the one on his forehead and had no swelling or darkening of the skin. He was called back again around half past one on Tuesday morning by two of Taylor's sons, when he suggested mustard plasters be applied, but he held out little hope for recovery. He was right – the next time the doctor saw Taylor was when he was performing a post-mortem on the deceased.

The post-mortem found Taylor to be quite a healthy man. Despite his heavy drinking, the heart, lungs, pancreas and kidneys were all reasonably healthy. On examining the head, the doctor found bruises with some internal bleeding but not extensive, nor was there any sign of any fracture of the skull. He did, however, find a massive blood clot weighing at least two ounces. In his opinion, the cause of death was the pressure of the clot of blood on the brain though he could find no rupture of it. The clot was not situated near any of the bruises but the doctor felt it might have come from concussion after a fall, probably though not certainly, from a blow at the back of the head. Heavy drinking could equally have caused the problem and even excessive excitability by the deceased could have caused a rupture of such a blood clot.

After this evidence, the coroner issued a warrant for Margaret Armstrong to be sent to trial for 'killing and slaying' Joseph Taylor. She appeared before the local magistrates – the Mayor, Mr Ridgway, the ex-Mayor, Mr J T Rawsthorne, and William Henry Thornton, MD. Bail, requested by her defence,

Mr Watts, was refused and she was sent to the assizes in Leeds.

In December, Armstrong appeared before the assize judges. In her defence she addressed the jury, confirming that she and Taylor 'lived together unhappily', saying that before she pushed him out of the house, he had grabbed hold of her and tried to hit her with a poker, which she had had to 'wrest' from him.

After reviewing all the evidence the jury found Armstrong guilty, but with a recommendation for mercy owing to provocation. She was sentenced to three months' imprisonment, with hard labour.

Ten years later, Margaret was still living in Whitworth Road with her youngest son, William, and both were working in local mills.

CHAPTER 13

Till Death Us Do Part: Dewsbury 1873

here was no doubt whatsoever that Peter Rhodes murdered his wife, but he was neither tried nor convicted for it.

On 12 March 1873 a jury assembled at the *White Swan Inn*, Earlsheaton, consisting of John Wilson, Henry Fenton, William Sykes, Thomas Audsley, Thomas Eastwood, Joseph Durford, John Tolson, Michael Preston, Robert Senior, Joseph Croft, H T Hemingway, William Waterhouse and Thomas Lee, the foreman. They had been brought together by the coroner, Thomas Taylor, to inquire into the death of Jane, the sixty-five-year-old wife of Peter Rhodes, a wood sawyer, originally from Ferrybridge, who lived on Commonside, Earlsheaton.

Their daughter, Frances Pearson, wife of William Pearson who was a shoemaker and keeper of the *Bricklayers' Arms* in Dewsbury, identified her mother's body, saying that she had seen them both the previous Saturday afternoon when they had visited her. They had both seemed on good terms with each other, both cheerful and happy because they each had received two shillings and sixpence (13p) from the local poor law Union.

Her mother easily got depressed, having been sent twice to the local asylum, once about twenty-seven years ago and again about five years ago. Both times she had tried to cut her own throat before being sent to the asylum.

Her sister-in-law, Elisabeth, confirmed that she too had seen the couple on the Sunday and both had been in good spirits.

On Monday 10 March, Peter Rhodes arrived at his daughter's house at about half past nine in the morning, telling Frances that her mother had gone on a visit to Morley with another relative, Mary Rhodes. He had already been to see her brother Thomas and his wife, Elisabeth. Peter seemed very strange.

Frances then noticed that he had some spots of blood on his face and asked him:

> *'What have you been doing to get all those clouts of blood on your face? Has your nose been bleeding?' He said it had and went into the kitchen to wipe his face. He then shook hands with his daughter and her husband and said he was going to the workhouse in the afternoon. Instead he went back to his son's house, simply informing his daughter-in-law, 'I've come to stay with you today, lass.' He then asked to lie down and spent the rest of the day asleep. When Thomas came home around half past five he went and looked at his father. Within minutes he had picked up his father's house key from the table where he'd put it and gone out.*

Frances received a message to go to her brother's house, but in fact she met him coming towards her on Malkroyd Lane. They went together to their parent's house in Earlsheaton. All was in darkness and the door was locked. Thomas unlocked it while Frances went for a candle from the next-door neighbour, Mary Preston, and they went in. At first they saw nothing amiss, but then Thomas saw something in the bed. He pulled off the covers and they saw the dead body of their mother, lying facing the wall. There was a big gash on the left side of her head.

Quickly they left, locking the door behind them and waited in Mary Preston's house until Constable Adams arrived. He and Thomas went back into the house, where Thomas showed the officer the body. There was blood all over her head, on the floor and on the wall. Adams locked the door again, leaving the key with the neighbour and set off for Thomas's house. There they found Peter Rhodes, still half asleep, and took him into custody.

In the meantime, Superintendent William Airton and Sergeant George Beevers went to the deceased's house. Nothing had been disturbed, and there appeared to be no sign of any struggle. In one corner of the room, Beevers found a hatchet, covered in blood and hair from the deceased woman. Airton returned to the police station in Dewsbury, by which time Peter Rhodes had been put in the office, pending the Superintendent's arrival. Rhodes was asleep but Airton woke him up and charged him with killing his wife. The man made no reply but seemed dazed. Airton spoke again, 'Do you understand what I say?' he asked. Rhodes shook his head, 'I don't understand,' he muttered. When the charge was repeated, he finally replied, 'I recollect nothing.'

The Superintendent took Rhodes' clothes away. There were no marks on the coat, but both the sleeves, the front and back of the shirt were spattered with blood. On removing his shoes and stockings in the cells, it was noted that he had a patch of blood at the top of the left foot.

Further investigation proved that the hatchet belonged to Jane Rhodes. Their next-door neighbour, Mary Lee, told the police that Jane and her husband came to live next door about ten months previously. They had always appeared very loving and where one went the other went too. On the Sunday morning she'd seen Peter Rhodes coming up the hill to his own house, with a striped rug over his shoulders. In a short time he came out with a blue rug over him and he went in the direction of Dewsbury. Mary Lee did not hear any noise in the house, either during the night or in the morning, but she did state that she had often seen Peter Rhodes chopping wood with the hatchet. Jane had told her the tool had belonged to her father.

At the inquest, James Cameron of Batley Carr, Physician and Surgeon, described what he found at the post-mortem. On the head was a comminuted fracture (fracture in which the bone is splintered into a number of small pieces) of left parietal bone (part of the skull bones). There was also an elliptical shaped wound on her face an inch below the angle of the lower jaw on the left side to within about two inches of the windpipe. Muscles, blood vessels and nerves were severed down to the spinal vertebrae. The rest of the body appeared quite healthy, so in his opinion the cause of death was haemorrhage from the wound in the neck, which was likely to have been produced by the edge of the hatchet. Heavy blows with the head of the hatchet probably produced the other two wounds. It was quite impossible that Jane Rhodes could have inflicted the injuries herself.

The coroner's jury had no option but to bring in a verdict of murder by Peter Rhodes, her husband.

However, that was not the only reason the jury had been empanelled.

Thomas Rhodes went on to describe his father. He was around seventy-two years old, he said, and a wood sawyer but had not been able to do this work for the last eighteen months. Instead, he and his wife had gone about hawking green groceries. At various times he, too, had been in the West Riding Asylum at Wakefield. The last time his wife had been in the asylum, Peter had become 'low spirited' and eventually Peter had been taken to the asylum as well where he remained about nine months. He and his wife had come out together. On the day of his mother's murder, Thomas described returning to his home with Constable Adams, obtaining a cab and going with the policeman and Peter Rhodes to the police station in Wellington Street. There he'd left his father asleep on

The old workhouse, Dewsbury. The author

the chair. On the following day he'd returned and seen his father in bed in a cell, still sleeping.

Superintendent Airton reminded the jury that he had searched Peter Rhodes when he'd been at the police station, finding some change, spectacles and a handkerchief, but nothing else.

It was then the turn of James Cameron, the surgeon. He stated that at about eleven o'clock on Monday 11 March he had seen Peter Rhodes in the receiving room at the police station. He had been seated on a chair apparently asleep. When the doctor examined him, he had noticed that Rhodes had a cold, clammy perspiration on the skin. His eyes were shut, and on raising the eyelids the doctor found the eyes fixed and the pupils contracted. The prisoner was breathing stertorously, with a very low pulse. He showed all the symptoms of having taken some narcotic. The man was removed to a cell and stimulants were given but he could not be roused. Dr Cameron said he saw him half a dozen times during the day but there was no change and by half past three

Dewsbury Cemetery. The author

in the afternoon, Peter Rhodes was dead. Cameron thought the narcotic was probably opium.

Emma Field, a neighbour from Earlsheaton, said that Rhodes had begun to be 'low' again before last Christmas. He had often told her that he would do away with himself rather than go again to the workhouse. Over the months since then he had gradually become weaker in body and mind.

The jury decided that Peter Rhodes had poisoned himself when of unsound mind.

On Thursday afternoon 'a large concourse of people assembled about the cottage where the deceased lived and in which their coffined bodies were lying'. The funeral procession, consisting of the hearse, shillibeer [type of omnibus], carriage, mourning coach and trap, set off accompanied by a throng of people. More lined Wellington Road, Webster Hill and the road leading up to Dewsbury Cemetery. The *Dewsbury Reporter* stated that 'a great majority of the people being women, young and old' with scarcely a man amongst them. After the short ceremony, all filed past the open grave where husband and wife were interred together.

CHAPTER 14

A Family Revenge: Doncaster 1828

In February 1828, John Dyon, a forty-year-old farmer who lived near Bawtry, Doncaster, was found with shot wounds in the chest and face.

The body was found by two of his workmen, John Hodgeson and Robert Farmery, who had been sent out to look for him. They helped move the body back to the farm and sent for the police and a doctor. At first they thought that robbery might have been the motive but Betty Dyon, his widow, who was nine months pregnant and later gave birth to a stillborn child, found his watch on his fob and a pocket

Crown Hotel, *Bawtry*. The author

St Helena's Church, Austerfield. The author

book with £28 in notes in his pocket, some silver in another pocket.

Within a very short time, Mr Timms, the police officer from Doncaster had traced footprints in the snow to the local village, where three or four individuals were initially arrested on suspicion of being involved, but on examination by the magistrate, Mr Denison, the evidence was so scanty that they were discharged.

Next, the man's own brother, William and nephew, John, were arrested and brought to the inquest which was held at the *Crown Inn*, Bawtry. Later they were released 'on their own recognizances' after Turner (son-in-law of William) stated that they were both at home at the time the murder was committed and the *Leeds Mercury* pointed out:

The two men – the undoubted perpetrators of the murder – who were seen near Mr Wagstaff's house, were totally different as to personal appearance from William Dyon and his son; nor does it appear to be possible that either of them could get on the boot or shoe worn by the actual murderer which from the impression in the snow is of fashionable shape, ten inches in length and only one and a half inches at the narrowest point.

These facts, as well as their general demeanour since suspicion has attached to them afford forcible presumptive proof that William Dyon and his son are guiltless of so horrid a crime. It is indeed revolting to the feelings to suppose that a brother and a nephew, after walking a number of miles, could, in the stillness of the night, coolly assassinate their relative from motives of pure revenge and without any apparent prospect of benefiting from his death.

John Dyon was interred at Austerfield on Wednesday 20 February, his killers still unknown.

The perpetrators, and the newspaper, reckoned without the diligence of Constable Etches, who continued his enquiries, even going so far as to fetch the magistrate from his bed to undertake a long journey to Gainsborough, where they stayed all day pursuing their enquiries. On Saturday morning, the brother and nephew of John Dyon were again arrested, taken to the *Crown Inn* at Bawtry and locked up. On Wednesday morning magistrates E H Denison, Rev Rudd, Rev E H Brooksbank and C Neville again called all their witnesses together for an initial trial. Turner now admitted that he had not told the truth and the Dyons were not, in fact, at home on the night in question.

The magistrate's examination took place in private, leaving the newspapers to glean what they could for their report. The editor of *Leeds Mercury* was most incensed, pointing out that:

The preceding account exhibits, in a strong point of view, not merely the inability but the mischief of private examination. In the absence of authenticated information, all the gossip of the neighbourhood will be retailed and in the present instance, a great number of particulars, most deeply criminating the accused parties, are avowedly stated to have for their basis, mere rumour. It is but common justice, therefore, to these unhappy men, to add that our readers cannot draw any conclusion from this statement

The Courthouse, York. The author

unfavourable to the accused without committed an act of the greatest injustice.

In April, the prisoners were brought before Baron Hullock, and a packed courtroom, at York. Counsel for the Prosecution were Messrs Sergeant Jones, Starkie, Hardy and Milner. Counsel for the Prisoners were Mr Williams and Mr Knowles; and 'gentlemen of the jury' were:

William Dean, of Scawsby in Ovenden, gent
John Donaldson, of Heworth, gent
John Ellis of Pickering, innkeeper
Thomas Elliot of Westcow, carpenter
John Foster, of Slack in Heptonstall, gent
Henry Gibson of High Street, Huddersfield, joiner
Thomas Hardcastle of Huntington, gent
John Johnson, of Osgodby, gent
John Key of Kirkgate, Bradford, druggist
Joshua Lea of Longroyd Bridge, Huddersfield, cotton dealer
Robert Leesley, Westgate, Rotherham, gent
John Levett, Ellerker, gent

First, the housing arrangements of the family were described. William Dyon was a farmer living at Morton Carr about one and a half miles from Gainsborough. The younger prisoner was his son, John, who boarded with his father, but slept at the house of his father-in-law, Mr Turner, who lived at Pulham Carr about three quarters of a mile from Morton Carr. Morton Carr is thirteen miles from Bancroft, where the murdered man lived. Turner's son, Robert, had married Sarah Dyon, daughter of elder prisoner, so he lived during the day with his father, and slept at night at his father-in-law's house.

William Wagstaff of Middlewood House told how he had met John Dyon on Saturday 16 February at Doncaster and returned home with him, leaving the town around 7 pm. Mr Broughton of Bawtry accompanied them as far as the lane that joins the Doncaster road with the Bawtry road, then Wagstaff and Dyon went on together on the Austerfield Lane. In going along this lane, the road lay within 200 yards of Partridge Hill, a farm tenanted by John Dyon. They parted at a place where Austerfield road joins the Bawtry and Thorne road, Dyon turning left and Wagstaff to the right. This was at about half-past eight. The defence cross-examined him about Dyon's attitude to poachers. Wagstaff agreed that Dyon 'did not like persons to trespass on his property'.

William Wright, surgeon from Bawtry said that he went to Dyon's house early on Sunday morning, arriving at about 5 am. Dyon was quite cold, the body appearing to have been dead six or seven hours. He found death caused by a gunshot wound, the ball having entered the chest on the left side under the second rib and passed through the lung. It had divided an artery and lodged just under the shoulder blade. This would have caused instant death. There were also some shot wounds to the face. The grey mare he was riding had also been wounded on the neck with shot.

John White was the next witness, but also considered an accessory to the murder. He had worked for the murdered man but prior to this, White had lived with the prisoner William Dyon at Morton Carr. It had been William who had recommended White to his brother. White lived at the farm at Partridge Hill, near the Austerfield lane, whilst John Dyon lived at Bancroft, about twelve miles away. Another farm servant, William Stacey, lived in the same house with White, together with their respective wives. White had not seen William Dyon for over a year until on the Friday night, 8 February, William and his son, John, came to Partridge Hill. White was in bed, but heard a knocking and opened the door to them. Both prisoners had smock frocks on and they both had guns, one being a long gun, the other a 'common sized' one. When White asked them what they were doing there, William first said they were come for some wild fowl shooting, then said they had not really come with that intent. William then asked if his brother was going to Doncaster next morning, Saturday. White said he didn't think so, but was sure to be going the Saturday after that since he never missed a fortnight. William then asked if they could leave the guns until they called again, but said they must be kept out of sight. White agreed and promised to take care of them. Despite being told that their real intent was to 'make away' with his employer, White continued to help the two men and failed to appear at the initial inquest, when these details should have been stated. William bribed the man with ten pounds if he kept quiet and the promise that he would take the tenancy of Partridge Hill farm and give it White when he inherited the Bancroft farm. He backed these statements up with a threat – that they would kill White too if he mentioned anything that they had said. White went to bed and left them in the kitchen, finding the guns in a corner of the room when he got up. He concealed them in the granary, under some straw. The following week, on Saturday 16 February he was returning from Bawtry and leading the horses down to the stables at about 7 pm when he saw the father and son again. White took them to the granary and gave them the guns, informing them that John Dyon was at Doncaster. William Dyon again said they were going to 'make away with him', repeating his threat to White if he said anything.

The Turner family, who were related by marriage to the Dyons, had originally said the prisoners had been at home on the night in question. Now Robert Turner said that he only saw the prisoners on Friday 8 February around eight or nine at night, but didn't see them after that, nor did he see them next day. On 16 February he went to Gainsborough and did not return to his father-in-law's at Morton Carr until seven in the evening. He did not see either of them before that time or before he went to bed, between eight or nine. In the middle of the night he heard something which may have been William Dyon coughing in one of the other rooms. Turner told the court that William Dyon had a long gun, which was kept in the cellar but he did not see it between 8 and 16 February, though this was not that unusual.

Robert's father, John, and John Dixon his servant confirmed the evidence of Robert Turner as to the absence of John and William from home on night of 8 February and afternoon of 16 February.

Sarah Hornsby was working at the farm in February and remembered the prisoners wanting their dinner early, as they were going out. They left the farm around two o'clock. She said they did not have smock frocks on when they left, though they were very common in the village.

The next witnesses traced the journey of the two prisoners from their own farm to that of the murdered man and back again. Samuel Marples said he crossed the river on the night in question with two men armed with guns and dressed in smock frocks, though he could not specifically identify them. John Cartwright, a labourer who lived at Misson, about a mile and a half from Bancroft, said he was working on the road on 8 February, when he saw William Dyon, with a young man, at about two o'clock on the road from Partridge Hill to Stockwith ferry. Dyon had a smock frock on.

Joseph Lundy of East Stockwith saw William Dyon and his son, both of whom he knew well, going from Morton Carr towards the ferry on Saturday 16 February. Both wore long smocks. He was sure it was William Dyon because of the way he turned his toes out very much in walking.

Ralph Driffield, also of Stockwith, also saw William and a young man that afternoon going towards the ferry.

William Holberry, ferryman at East Stockwith, remembered taking William Dyon across on Friday or Saturday 15 or 16, with a young man. Holberry also ferried two men across on the 8 February at about ten at night from Lincolnshire to Yorkshire, but said he did not know them. George Vernon and Samuel Marples were in the boat at the same time.

On the opposite bank, William Barnett saw the prisoners at Stockwith on 16 February, coming from the ferry and going along Bickerdike Lane at about half past two or three. They were going towards Idlestock, on the road to Bancroft where the murder was committed. William Loveday, a labourer, was in a field a mile and a half from Bancroft, between two and three o'clock. At about three o'clock he saw a man in a dirty smock frock in a turnip field near that in which he was working. A little after he saw the first man, he saw two men enter the plantation near the field which borders on Deeps Lane. He left around four o'clock before they went away.

William Broadbent, a workman in employ of Mr Wagstaff, saw two men coming from the direction of Stockwith ferry towards Bancroft about 4 pm and James Brooks saw two men loitering on the afternoon in question within three-quarters of a mile of Partridge Hill.

William Loveday (not the first one of that name) of Misson said he too had been out on 16 February. As he was returning home through Richardson's Lane near Deeps Lane between 8 and 9 pm, he heard the sound of two guns, so close together he could scarcely distinguish one from the other. It was a still night and frosty. Just after he heard the gunshot he met Mr Wagstaff, returning from the Doncaster market.

Thomas Tew who lived at West Stockwich, owned a boat about twenty feet long. At about 11 pm on Saturday 16 February, it was lying high and dry but next morning it was lying high and dry on the opposite side of the river. It must have been taken across when the tide was high at about 11 pm from its position on the opposite bank. One man could not move the boat into the water, he said.

Joseph Jaques, a shepherd who worked for the late Mr Dyon, examined the ground the morning after the murder:

The evidence of this witness was very long, minute and related entirely to tracing footsteps. The footsteps of two men were marked on the snow up to the place of the murder and to some distance from it but they were not traced nearer to Partridge Hill than half a mile. The footsteps of one of the men were remarkable from the degree in which the toes were turned out and this corresponded with a peculiarity in William Dyon's walk.

The magistrate, Edward Beckett Denison, also went to the spot on Sunday morning and looked at the footsteps nearest the place where Dyon shot. These were sixteen feet from the gate. He was able to confirm Jaques' testimony. He was also questioned regarding White's evidence. Denison said that the £100 guineas reward was offered on Tuesday or Wednesday after the murder, but White did not give his account of the transaction till the 10 March. That account was not voluntary, though Denison omitted to say how the account had been obtained.

Rev John Rudd, also one of the committing magistrates, said that William Dyon was examined in the absence of his son and had told them that he had been thrashing in the early part of the afternoon and that he had been warping with his son John in the afternoon. John Dyon was then examined and said he'd not been warping at all that afternoon.

Williamson Etches, constable, of Doncaster, produced a long gun, used for shooting wild ducks, found in the cellar of William Dyon. When the two men had first been arrested, Etches had taken their boots and shoes, but these had been returned when they were discharged and could not now be found.

The defence was minimal. The Staceys, who lived at Partridge Hill, said they did not remember being disturbed on any night in February but also admitted that they slept at the front of the house, the White's at the back, so it was not surprising that they had heard nothing. The two prisoners said nothing in their defence.

All that was lacking was a motive.

John Wilson came forward to say that he had been coming from Lincoln Fair last April. William Dyon overtook him and in the course of the conversation had said his brother John was a damned rogue but he would be as good as him some day. Samuel Kilsey said he was at the *Nag's Head* in Gainsborough with John Jun about three weeks ago. John had said that his grandfather had left his uncle £30,000 and his father very little but 'he would see how it should be done'. Kilsey had told him to hold his tongue for the less was said about such matters the better.

Next, John Baines produced a deed by which John Dyon the elder, the father of William and grandfather of the younger prisoner, made over the greater part of the landed property to John Dyon, his second son. The land consisted of about sixty-three acres. Baines was a witness to the deed. The personal property was also made over to John Dyon. No reason was given for this.

This seemed to be sufficient for the jury. The judge summed up, during which he made the comment:

> *I am sure ... that it is quite unnecessary either for you or me to advert to any reports which may have appeared in the newspapers or circulated in other ways; you will confine your attention strictly to the evidence which has been laid before you this day and on it alone you will form your judgements.*

The jury retired for all of six minutes before returning to pronounce both prisoners guilty. They were sentenced to death by hanging and their bodies to be delivered to the surgeons for dissection.

The pair insisted they were innocent, despite all efforts of the Chaplain of the Castle, Rev William Flower. On the Tuesday morning, they attended services at the chapel but it was only after the second service that the young man was heard to exclaim, 'Oh, what have we brought ourselves to!'

At the time of the execution, crowds of people lined Fishergate, St George's Field and other streets around the castle. The clergyman said prayers, young John Dyon joining in the service fervently but William remained unmoved. At the point of execution, the Under Sheriff, John Brook, asked them again whether they admitted their guilt. John exclaimed, 'Oh, yes,' but William said nothing.

CHAPTER 15

An Excessively Cruel Act: Doncaster 1866

At Rossington, near Doncaster, Messrs Smith, Knight & Co were the contractors given the job of building the Doncaster to Gainsborough railway. To do this they needed a labour force and the cheapest workers were Irish navvies, many of whom brought their families with them.

Ten-year-old Frederick Mason managed to find his own employment, keeping the crows off the crops for a local farmer. On Sunday 11 March he set off for work, taking with him a couple of companions, Patrick, aged five and his little sister, Margaret, aged three, children of Christopher Davies, who was working on the railway.

For some reason, that afternoon, Frederick suddenly began to beat the two little children with a stick until they were almost unconscious. He then threw them into the River Torn, but the cold water seemed to revive them and they began to cry. He pulled them out again, but again he beat them with the stick and threw them back into the water. This time Patrick didn't cry out, just held his sister's head above the water, which fortunately wasn't very deep, until Frederick had gone away. After that, the little lad cried out for help and George Crosby who was working nearby heard him. He and some of the other navvies came to their rescue, pulling the little girl clear of the mud and taking the children back to their father's house. PC Cowan was sent for and he instructed the parents to give the girl dilute brandy and rub her with salt until the

Headline, Leeds Mercury, *1866.* Author's collection

ATTEMPTED DOUBLE MURDER BY A BOY.

doctor, John Lister, arrived. He found the children in a very poorly state, both suffering numerous deep cuts about the head. Patrick was almost unconscious and for a while it was feared that he would not survive. Little Margaret was unable to speak at first, but eventually was able to tell them of Mason's actions.

When Constable Cowan arrested Mason he seemed quite unconcerned and admitted that he had done exactly what the little girl had said. The lad appeared before the local magistrates and was remanded in custody to appear at the next assizes.

He appeared before Justice Shee in April and the jury listened carefully to the evidence, which included the fact that Frederick was an 'ill-behaved' boy and had been thrown out of school just a fortnight before because of his behaviour. In mitigation, his defence solicitor, Mr Woodhead, said he had drunk a pint of beer earlier on in the day and had then gone on to share, with three other lads, a half gallon of ale and gin. However, Dr Lister stated that when he saw Mason two hours after the attack, the lad was perfectly sober.

The judge then informed them they had to consider two questions: whether the prisoner had committed the offence with the intent to do the children grievous bodily harm; and whether at the time he had acted with a guilty knowledge of doing wrong.

The jury retired for only fifteen minutes before delivering a verdict of 'guilty of inflicting grievous bodily harm'.

The judge sentenced Mason to fourteen days' imprisonment and afterwards to be confined in a reformatory for five years. He remarked that if Mason had been a man he would have received a much more severe punishment.

CHAPTER 16

A Seaman in the Dock: Goole
1896

Early in 1895 Emma, younger daughter of John and Sarah Womack married Joseph, the younger son of Robert and Mary Ellis. The Ellis family were all mariners, plying their boats up and down the Knottingley-Goole canal. Both families had come to Goole from the Knottingley and Brotherton area, living just a few streets apart and probably knew each other well.

By the beginning of 1896, life had seemed just perfect to Emma. She had her little boy, Herbert, to look after and a handsome young husband; though it was true they had their arguments.

But things gradually got worse, and she finally returned to her parent's house in Back George St, Clegg's Yard, Goole. Towards the end of June, she and her husband officially separated and he agreed to pay her five shillings (25p) a week in maintenance.

On 1 July, Joseph sent a little girl to the house with five shillings for his wife. Soon after he arrived at the Womack's house, asking her to sign a receipt for the five shillings he had sent to her, which she did. On handing the paper back to him, he suddenly grabbed her round the neck and stabbed her twice. Emma managed to break free, rushing out of the house into that of a neighbour's, Mrs Broadhead. Her mother followed her. A few minutes later, the door burst open and Joseph appeared, chasing Emma out of the house. He caught her under the archway at the end of the yard, furiously stabbing at his wife's left side again, holding her by the left shoulder while he 'hammered her back with the knife' which eventually broke apart. She collapsed onto the roadway. Emma was taken to the cottage hospital in Goole.

When George Huntingdon came out of the *Mariner's Arms* later in the day, he saw Joseph sharpening a knife on a stone wall. Suddenly Joseph went towards George, sawing and hacking at his own throat, saying that he was no threat to anyone else except any of his own family. Huntingdon took the knife off him. Joseph was arrested and also taken to the cottage hospital where Dr Grainger Brown treated him for his injuries. During the night, Joseph had some sort of a fit but recovered. He appeared to repent of his actions, asking the doctor to see his wife and ask her to forgive him. Despite her injuries, Emma forgave her husband just hours before she died.

The inquest was arranged for the Saturday, at the *Sydney Hotel*, Goole, when Dr Blair told the coroner that Emma's death had been the result of three wounds in the side that had penetrated the lungs. Emma's mother, Sarah Womack, had also been attacked so was not able to attend the inquest, which was adjourned to enable her to recover and attend to give her evidence. The coroner's court sent Joseph to the assizes.

At Joseph's later trial in Leeds before Justice Kennedy, Dr Brown suggested that the attack might have been the result of 'impulsive insanity' but could not explain how this differed from simple rage. It was possible, he thought, that the inflammation of the eye, for which he had been treating Joseph, could have 'communicated to the brain'. Joseph's defence did not try to plead insanity, but did suggest that the young man had been provoked so much by his wife and her family that the charge should be manslaughter not murder. On questioning Sarah Womack, she did admit that on at least one occasion, Joseph had got up to find his wife away from the house, no fire in the grate and nothing to eat but a bit of cake. The Womack family had often used 'strong language' to the man, but Sarah denied she had frequently used 'coarse language' to imply infidelity on the part of the prisoner. The jury agreed that the prisoner had had some provocation, pronouncing him guilty, but pleaded for mercy. This still did not save Joseph from the gallows.

James Billington, executioner, arrived at Armley Gaol on 25 August. He had allowed a drop of seven feet nine inches to be sure of instant death. At 9 am Joseph Ellis was executed.

There quickly followed an inquest by Mr Malcolm, the city coroner who heard the evidence of J H Shepherd, governor of the prison; E R Dodsworth, acting Deputy Sheriff, and Mr Moynihan the prison surgeon. The inquest jury simply agreed that the sentence had been duly carried out.

The little boy, Herbert, was brought up by his grandparents, John and Sarah Womack.

CHAPTER 17

Attempted Murder: Pollington 1870

Mary had been brought up in the village of Pollington, about ten miles from Goole, working as a dairymaid at a local farm. She married and moved away to Leeds, but separated from her husband and returned, with her little boy, John, to live with her parents. Her father, John Bellwood, who had worked as a general labourer, was by now working on the Knottingley to Goole Canal, in charge of the turn bridge that provided a means for pedestrians to cross the canal on their route to Sykehouse.

In the summer of 1869 she began seeing Robert Bradley, an ex-soldier who had been something of a hero. He had been in India during the Indian Mutiny, rescued two children from the

Aire & Calder Navigation at Pollington, where the swing bridge used to be.
The author

Headline, Goole Times *1870.*
Author's collection

CUTTING A WOMAN'S THROAT AT
POLLINGTON, BY A GOOLE LABOURER.
ESCAPE OF THE PRISONER.

massacre of Cawnpore and earned himself almost £100 in prize money (extra payments to soldiers) for his services to his country. By the beginning of 1870 the relationship was becoming serious. In fact, Bradley told her that he had been to London and obtained a divorce for Mary and that they could now get married. She was not quite so keen.

On 19 January Bradley stayed overnight with the Bellwood family, arranging to leave very early the next morning. Mary got up to prepare his breakfast. Bradley repeated his proposal of the previous evening, saying he wanted to get married on Friday, which Mary considered to be an unlucky day. After breakfast, the pair left the house, Mary taking the key for the bridge-lock in order to operate the swing bridge. Bradley opened the little garden gate and she went before him, remarking that there was a small steamer on the canal. Just as she reached the bridge-lock, Bradley seized her under the chin, dragging her head back and slashing at her throat with a razor, held in his right hand. She tried desperately to call for help, but when she grasped his hand to pull it away from her chin he cut her across her fingers. Finally she managed to break free and her screams brought her mother out of the house. Bradley ran off down the lane.

Dr Thompson was called in, finding a two-inch long wound across Mary's throat. Though fairly superficial, it was in a dangerous place and she could easily have lost her life.

Sergeant Thomas set off to find Bradley, following a trail of drops of blood along the side of the canal as far as Rawcliffe Bridge. The blood trail then ceased and, at first, it was thought that Bradley might have tried to cut his own throat then thrown himself into the canal, but within a few hours he was found alive and well. He could give no reason for his actions, merely stating that he had thrown the razor into one of the many dykes around that area.

The local magistrates had no difficulty in deciding to send him to Leeds for trial at the next Assizes.

In March, Bradley appeared before Sir Montague Edward Smith. The prosecution was led by Mr Wheelhouse who stated that the twenty-three-year-old sail maker had two charges against him (presumably to make sure he could be convicted of at least one of them). The first stated that he had wounded Mary Hawley with intent to murder, the second that he had wounded her with intent to do her grievous bodily harm. He said he had only intended 'to frighten her'. This time his defence was that Mary had threatened to murder him and had, in fact, pushed him into the canal. She denied any such action and the jury decided her version of events was the truth. Their decision was that Bradley was guilty of wounding with intent to murder.

The judge told Bradley that they 'could not possibly come to any other conclusion…because you used an instrument calculated to take the woman's life, and it was as nearly taken as possible'.

Since the crime was as near to murder as could be Bradley was sentenced to ten years in prison.

CHAPTER 18

Murder at Wadsworth: Halifax 1858

O n Thursday 14 January 1858 William Shackleton looked across the bleak wildness of the moors near his farm and muttered over his farmhand's poor workmanship. He had asked the man to shift manure into the fields, but there, in the wrong place, was a pile of black manure. He waited all day for his worker to go and shift it, but finally at four o'clock he went to investigate for himself.

Instead of manure, he found the mutilated body of a man, parts of his coat in shreds from the frenzied slashing with a knife and his throat was sliced through. His right eye was completely black and there was a long gash across his

Hare & Hounds Inn, *near Hebden Bridge*. The author

forehead. His skull, just behind the right ear, was crushed with some rough item such as a large stone. There was a smaller, similar wound on the left, where his ear had also been cut almost completely off. There were a number of puncture wounds into his chest and the whole of his upper body and head were covered in small stab wounds.

Halifax Town Hall. The author

Shackleton went for help, going first to William Greenwood's farm as he thought the man might have been Greenwood's cousin. Shackleton, William and Miles Greenwood returned, searching the area for possible weapons. William Greenwood found a broken blade of an ordinary carving knife and a large copingstone near the man's head, which had obviously been used to smash his skull, as there were the remains of blood and hair on it. After the parish constable, Mr Parker and Inspector Nicholson arrived, the body was removed to the *Hare and Hounds Inn* nearby. Soon the body was identified as Bethel Parkinson, a farmer and dealer who lived at *Raggald's Inn*, near Queensbury.

The inquest, on the following Saturday, before George Dyson began at the *Hare and Hounds*, when the body was formally identified. It was then adjourned until the following Friday at the *White Horse Inn*, Hebden Bridge. The body was described as:

> ... *bruised and hacked in this horrible manner, yet the dead man's arm was raised and immovably fixed in its position, as if, even in the awful fixity of death, he would yet protect himself from his pitiless destroyer.*

By the time the adjourned inquest reassembled, the police had arrested a young man named Joseph Shepherd, who had been taken before the magistrates at Halifax Town Hall and remanded in custody. Shepherd, a gentleman's servant, had been employed as a cab driver for John Lynch of Halifax but was currently unemployed. He had also recently separated from his wife and was living with his father, Robert, at Holdsworth, near Halifax. When the police arrived with their prisoner at Hebden Bridge they were greeted with a large mob that hooted and yelled at the man.

Joseph Mann, also known as Doud o'Manuel's, told the inquest that Bethel Parkinson was his son-in-law, having married his daughter Mary in 1850. Mann saw Parkinson with Joseph Shepherd outside his house at *Raggald's Inn* on the Wednesday. His last sighting had been of the pair of them in Bradshaw Lane. Later Shepherd had been seen washing blood from a pair of trousers. Further evidence suggested that he had lately obtained a sum of money, which was quite enough for the jury to return a verdict of wilful murder and send him to York for trial.

On March 20, Shepherd came before Justice Byles; Mr Overend, Mr Vernon Blackburn and Mr Maule were for the prosecution and Mr Price was assigned by the judge for the defence.

The jury consisted of:

Matthew Balmforth, Aislaby; James Duffield, Aldbrough; James Forman, Goole; Patrick Aitchison, Sheffield; John Stancliffe, Huddersfield; Jacob Baxindall, Alberton; William Tummond Burton, Doncaster; George Emmerson, Wakefield; Edward Shields, Boroughbridge; Thomas Thistle, Aislaby; George Ingold Torr, Beverley; and George Wilson, Aldborough.

Shepherd, who was described as a 'good looking young man of fair complexion but rather effeminate appearance' pleaded not guilty.

The route the two men had taken was traced with the help of a variety of witnesses. Joseph Mann saw them at Bradshaw

Raggald's Inn, *Queensbury.* The author

Lane End, then Hannah Garth, whose husband Samuel was the toll bar keeper at *Raggald's Inn* saw Shepherd and Parkinson together, and spoke to Parkinson. Joseph Mitchell saw the two men together near Parkinson's home and saw them go through the toll bar around 1 pm. Next at around 2 pm, John Priestley, a labourer, saw them in Taylor Lane, Delph going towards Cockhill Gate, where they were seen at 2.45 pm by Samuel Jowitt. By 3 pm they were seen by Jonathan Wilson at Ratten Clough. Solomon Farnell, a shopkeeper at Lane Head, Ovenden stated that Shepherd had come into his shop to buy some parkin, but as he didn't have any the man bought a plain cake and some cheese. A little later Jonathan Radcliffe of Goose Clough, Ovenden saw Shepherd and Parkinson together walking across the fields. One of them was eating something.

Hannah Hodgson was visiting her sister, Mercy Greenwood, at Low Farm and saw the two men trespassing across their fields and watched them climbing over three walls before heading off towards Cold Edge. Both were young men and quite small in stature. William Greenwood, of Wadsworth, saw the two men go over the hill towards Wadsworth Moor, where Parkinson's body was found.

On the day before the murder, Shepherd had been at the *White Horse* inn in Halifax, where he had offered the ostler, Thomas Holliday, a carving knife for sale. It had a black handle and a drawing of a hare and hounds carved into the blade. The ostler refused to buy it, saying it was a dangerous weapon to carry about. Later, Shepherd was seen with Parkinson discussing the sale of cattle from the farm of a recently deceased farmer. Parkinson asked George Normington (or Normanton), his brother-in-law, to lend him thirty shillings to buy some animals, but was refused. That Wednesday morning, Parkinson asked his wife Mary to lend him two sovereigns, which she did before she went off to her work as a weaver in the Black Dyke Mills of Queensbury.

At 7pm, William Greenwood of High Royd, weaver, met a man coming from the direction of Common Farm where the body was found. The man asked him the way to Luddenden Foot Station. Shortly after, a man dressed as the prisoner had

Black Dyke Mills, Queensbury. The author

been dressed, ran into Luddenden station, bought a second class ticket to Halifax, and jumped on the train just as it was about to leave. At Halifax, Shepherd hitched a lift from a cabman named William Birch, whom he knew well, and went into a 'house of ill-repute' owned by a Mrs Eastwood.

Two girls, Mary Gordon and Sarah Hay, let him in and he gave Mary a gold sovereign to fetch some sherry for them all. When she returned, he asked for hot water and a sponge, which was when she noticed blood on his trousers, and also on his hands and fingernails. He said he had been fighting. He described himself as a 'blackguard' but assured the frightened girl he wouldn't harm her. He then changed his mind about the trousers, left the house but returned about half an hour later, with his trousers wet and scrubbed. Mary told him there was still blood on him but he brushed aside her comment about murdering someone and ordered supper.

He swore then that he would burn the trousers and buy new ones, despite the fact that they were good quality. He was also heard to say that he didn't have long to live, so was determined

Railway Station, Halifax. The author

to enjoy what was left of his life. He asked the two girls to go with him to Huddersfield the next day and sent for another cabbie friend called Charles Ramsden, to whom he gave another sovereign for the cab hire. The four of them stayed drinking all night, consuming three bottles of sherry. The two girls accompanied him to bed, though they insisted that Shepherd got into bed and they merely lay on the covers, still partially dressed.

The next morning Sarah Hay commented on the first falls of snow, to which Shepherd replied, 'That will just suit me.' The prosecution were at pains to point out that this was because the snow would delay the finding of the body. Shepherd left the house supposedly to fetch the cab but never returned. He met two friends, Isaac Sutcliffe and William Dickenson, whom he treated to some drinks at the *All Nations* pub. They noticed blood on his clothes and this time the tale was that he had been in a slaughterhouse. On Thursday night he treated another friend to some drinks, seeming to have plenty of money, though no one knew where it had come from.

The police arrived at his father's house on Saturday but failed to find Shepherd. On his return, his father, Robert Shepherd, asked him why the police were looking for him, but Joseph said he had done nothing wrong. His father told him to give himself up to the police, which Joseph did – but stopped to put on some different corduroy trousers, belonging to one of his brothers. He took his own to a coke oven at the coal mine at Catherine Slack where he asked the fireman, Laurence Chatburn, if he could throw a bundle into the ovens. After doing this he turned to the man and asked him if he was sure 'It will never be seen any more?' Once reassured on this point, he continued to the police station.

He told the police he had last seen Bethel Parkinson on Tuesday, though witnesses had seen them together on Wednesday. Shepherd was wearing a black cloth cap, black jacket and waistcoat and clogs. All the witnesses said the man they had seen with Parkinson had been wearing black. The stranger who had asked directions to Luddenden Station had been wearing a checked red and black scarf, which corresponded with the one Shepherd was wearing.

On searching his father's house, the police found a white handled carving knife complete with engraving of a hare and hounds. Robert Shepherd admitted that it was one of a pair, the other black handled one had been missing a few days. He also confirmed that the trousers Joseph had been wearing belonged, in fact, to a younger brother, Taylor.

The defence tried to cast doubt on the witnesses, pointing out that not all had positively identified Shepherd as the man with Parkinson, merely said that it was probably him, though they were all at a considerable distance from the men. Shepherd also knew that Parkinson had failed to borrow the thirty shillings (£1.50) he'd expected so it was unreasonable for him to have murdered the man for the small amount he had on him. The two girls were dismissed as completely unreliable in view of their profession, since 'over their minds no moral obligation to society existed' (*The Times*). They'd said they were frightened, that the man looked like a murderer, yet they had spent the evening drinking with him and slept the night in his bed. The handle of the knife had not been found so it could not be sworn that it was definitely the one that had belonged to the prisoner's father, nor could it be proved that it was a pair of bloody trousers Shepherd had burnt in the coke ovens. And anyway, he didn't look like a murderer.

The judge had difficulty summing up, stressing that the prisoner must be given the benefit of the doubt, but that most evidence was likely to be circumstantial because murder was generally done without witnesses. The jury must decided if the facts pointed to the prisoner's guilt or to his innocence. It took just thirty minutes for the jury to return and give their verdict: guilty. The judge then pronounced sentence of death.

On Saturday 3 April, Shepherd's hanging was the spectacle of the day, with over 10,000 people there. Unlike most prisoners Shepherd displayed neither remorse nor fear, nor would he confess his guilt. Just two days before the hanging he was calmly telling the gaoler that he would like a good 'blow-out' (dinner) before he was hanged, that he would rather be shot than hanged and that he was glad the weather was fine as he would rather be hanged in summer than winter. He also threatened to kick the hangman off the scaffold.

The hangman in question was Thomas Askern from Rotherham. He had at one time been in prison himself for debt but was released after he agreed to become hangman, carrying out hangings not just at York but at Leeds, Durham and other places in the north. When Shepherd was brought up to the scaffold at noon, his head was already covered with the white cloth, perhaps because of the threats he had made to the executioner.

The crowd fell silent as the noose was carefully draped over the prisoner's head and his last words were 'Lord, have mercy on me.' Some of the men in the watching crowd actually fainted as the young man was launched into eternity. Shepherd was buried in the precincts of the Castle.

CHAPTER 19

The Killing of Ellen: Heckmondwike 1868

On Monday 23 October, Henry Calvert, a collier, was brought to the Court House in Dewsbury, before magistrates J B Greenwood, Thomas F Firth, William Carr and W Crowther, on a charge of killing his wife.

The court heard the evidence that had been produced at the coroner's inquest, held at the *Cross Keys* in Liversedge on the previous Monday, before Thomas Taylor.

Mary, wife of Benjamin Ord, said that for last twelve weeks Henry Calvert and his wife, Ellen, had lived next door to her in Quaker Lane, Liversedge. On Thursday 15 October, she

Cross Keys Inn, *Liversedge*. The author

saw Ellen in Cleckheaton, fit and well. On the same day, about teatime, Henry had asked if Mary had seen his wife.

When Mary replied that she had, he said, 'I'll find her if I can but I don't want her to live with me. I would rather have the woman I have.'

Mary told him, 'Now, Harry, whatever thou does, do not touch her.'

He replied, 'I'll not promise but I'll talk to her nicely and get her home and then I'll give her it and if I get hold of Colly, then I'll poise them both to death.'

Kelita Richardson of Adwalton, a coalminer whose nickname was Colly, admitted that he knew Ellen Calvert. About four years previously he had lodged with them for a few weeks, and recently gone to lodge with them again. Henry Calvert was not too pleased about this arrangement, and with good reason. On Sunday 4 October, Ellen and Kelita had absconded together to Leeds. They had hoped to find work, but when that failed they went to Wakefield, then on to Adwalton.

On Friday 16 October, Kelita had got home from work and gone to the pub. A little while later, Ellen came in with her husband. Henry said he wanted her to come and collect her youngest child, as he could not keep it quiet, but Ellen made it clear she would not go with him, saying she would rather go twelve months in prison than go with him. Henry then said her parents had sent him as her mother was dead. This changed Ellen's mind and they all returned to the lodgings. Calvert had seemed to want Kelita to go with them to help her fetch the child back, telling him to get washed and Ellen found him a clean shirt. Kelita told him he'd rather not go and that she might either stop or come back as he (Calvert) had a mind. Shortly after this, Ellen went out and Calvert followed her, seemingly talking agreeably together. Calvert seemed to be calm and sober all the time. Kelita commented on the fact that Calvert was wearing a pair of wooden clogs, which were worn at the toes and had no iron on them.

Edwin Thornton, a machine maker from Liversedge, saw Calvert and Ellen on the footpath to Gomersal on Friday afternoon, near Popeley Farm. The woman seemed to be stooping, with Calvert standing in front of her but not

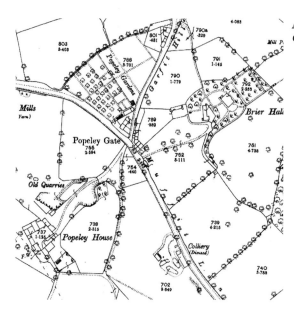

Map of Popeley Farm, Gomersal. The author

touching her. Thornton stopped and talked with Thomas Balmforth in a field about 150 yards from the pair, watching them for over ten minutes, obviously concerned. He saw the man take hold of the woman's arm and assist her gently into next field, but she walked back and laid herself down. When the man returned and looked at her, Thornton and his companion went up to them, asking what was wrong. The woman seemed to be almost unconscious, but Calvert explained that she was poorly, he thought she was having a miscarriage, but he had no money to send for assistance. Thornton then went to the nearest farmer, Jonas Seed and brought back a horse and cart. Carefully they put the woman into the cart and Seed drove the Calverts home. Though Thornton had been concerned, he admitted that he had not heard any screaming or signs of violence.

On arrival at Liversedge, their neighbour, Eliza Hutton came to help them, watching as they carried Ellen into the house, which the *Leeds Mercury* described as 'a wretched structure, most miserably furnished and exceedingly dirty.' She asked Calvert if he had beaten her, to which he replied, 'No but I pushed her over a low wall and she has hurt herself.'

He told her he had been for a doctor but one wasn't in and the other wouldn't come. Eliza told Henry to go again for the doctor, or at least for Ellen's sister or brother. Henry set off and returned over thirty minutes later with Ellen's elder brother, Robert. It was too late. She was already dead.

Ellen's brother, Robert Benson, confirmed his sister's age as thirty-four years. He explained that their mother had suffered paralysis for four or five years, which would be why Ellen had quickly agreed to return with Calvert, but their mother was not, in fact, dead. Ellen had married Henry Calvert eleven years ago. When Henry arrived at his house, at about seven o'clock on Friday night, Robert had asked why he was needed. Henry replied, 'I believe I've killed your Ellen.'

As they were walking, Henry had said to him that he had shoved Ellen against a wall in some close on White Lee Road.

Sergeant William Lund and Constable Hellawell, who took Calvert into custody, returned to White Lee Road, finding the place where Ellen had laid down covered in blood. There were signs nearby of some sort of a struggle.

John Ellis, surgeon, assisted by Dr Bennet of Cleckheaton performed the post-mortem. All the internal organs were healthy, though she was very emaciated and there was only one sign of violence on the body. This was a severe bruise on the abdomen such as could have been produced by a blow with a blunt, heavy instrument or violent kick. The deceased was three months pregnant. Internally there was a two-inch long wound through the pubic artery and vein, the cause of death being haemorrhage from the ruptured blood vessels. They were of the opinion that after such rupture a woman might live for about two or three hours, and her life could possibly have been saved if a medical man had been called in immediately.

The magistrates committed Calvert to the assizes in Leeds on a charge of wilful murder.

In December he appeared before Justice Brett. Mr Shaw and Mr Cadman prosecuted; Mr Vernon Blackburn defended. The *Huddersfield Examiner* described the prisoner as: 'below average height, about thirty-two years old … and has a most repulsive and unintelligent countenance.'

YORKSHIRE GAOL DELIVERY.

WEST RIDING DIVISION.

LEEDS TOWN HALL, MONDAY.
(Before Mr. Justice BRETT.)
ALLEGED WIFE MURDER NEAR DEWSBURY.
HENRY CALVERT (32), collier, was charged with the
wilful murder of Ellen Calvert, at Birstal, on the 16th
October.—Mr. SHAW and Mr. CADMAN were for the prose-

Headline, Leeds Mercury, *1868.*
Author's collection

By this time, Calvert had seen fit to make a full confession to Police Superintendent Parker, as he had 'not a friend in the whole world'. He corroborated the evidence given by the other witnesses at the inquest and magistrate's hearing, saying that when he had seen her in Adwalton, he had reminded her that she had three little children at home and she should be with them. She had replied that:

If she thought she was bound to live with me any more, she would poison me. I kicked her on the back. She then said I had caused her to miscarry . . . I did not think I should be the cause of my wife's death. (The Times)

The judge pointed out that there was no one who actually saw what had really happened that night on the footpath. It was on a public path, not a secret place. He seemed to have no intention to kill her, but he had given her a brutal and violent kick that had been sufficient to cause so much internal bleeding as to kill her. Yet he did not feel that this was sufficient for wilful murder. Both prosecution and defence agreed that they would accept a verdict of manslaughter and this was the final decision. Justice Brett then passed a sentence of twenty years' penal servitude.

The children were initially taken into the care of their neighbour, Mrs Ord, but were later brought up by their relatives.

CHAPTER 20

Murderous Assault at Shelley: Huddersfield
1866

William Leather came out of the workhouse in 1865 with no place to go. His mother, Hannah, had recently died and no one else in the family wanted him. Eventually, his mother's sister, Lucy Thornton, took him in, allowing him to sleep in her parlour in the hope that he would do odd jobs around the house. After all, she was well over seventy and, although she still did all her own housework and even worked filling bobbins for looms, she could always use an extra pair of hands around the house. Her husband, James, had died a few years previously, though her son and daughter still lived in the neighbourhood, as did other nephews and nieces – the whole family had lived in the Kirkburton area for a number of generations.

But William liked his drink. Not only that, but he liked to stay out late with his friends. On Monday 15 January around six o'clock, William made his way from his work to the *Gardeners Arms* at Shelley. Amos Ramsden, the innkeeper, knew him well, serving him with some tobacco and three gills of ale, roughly the equivalent of a pint. William had very little money, so this was all he had to drink, spreading it out over the evening. Ramdsen served him nothing else after about half past seven, but William stayed in the inn with his friends, chatting and enjoying himself. It was well after midnight when he left.

During the day, Lucy Thornton had pottered around her house and gone up to her daughter's at least three times as was quite usual – they only lived a hundred yards apart. At four o'clock, she went home, but was out again at six – this time to visit her nephew, George Robinson and his family, with whom she regularly 'ate her bacon'. She was a redoubtable old lady, reasonably healthy but a bit overweight and frequently complaining of indigestion. She also complained about William coming in late.

By nine o'clock on Monday night, Lucy was in bed. At half past twelve, William arrived home, knocking on the door to be let in. Perhaps she didn't hear him or perhaps it took her longer than William liked for her to get to the door, but the pair quarrelled violently.

Next morning, William went to another neighbour, Ann and John Shaw, asking if they could take him in as a lodger as Lucy had hit him four or five times with the fire poker for being late. John said to him, 'Are thou stalled where thou art?' to which William replied,

'Yes, old Luce and I have fallen out and I have picked her down.'

He said nothing more, but got his breakfast with them and then left. His belongings consisted of only a pair of old breeches, a shirt, an old bed quilt and some bread. When he

Police station, Kirkburton. The author

returned at dinnertime, he complained that he had found his day's work difficult because of pain where Lucy had struck him on the chest.

During the day, nothing had been heard or seen of Lucy and by teatime her daughter, Hannah, was getting worried. She sent her little girl, Ellen, who was only ten, to see how the old lady was. Within minutes Ellen was back, crying that her grandmother was lying in a pool of blood and couldn't move. Hannah rushed back to the cottage, finding her mother lying on the floor with just her chemise and nightgown on. There was no fire and the chair was tipped up. She was cold and helpless, her face and arms covered with blood. Hannah called in the neighbours, Ann Fitton and Mary Green, who helped her to lift her mother into bed. It was Ann Fitton who found the poker, hidden under the blood soaked blankets. There was a massive wound over the old woman's right eye and three strange wounds on her right arm, as if a savage dog had worried it. The nephew, George, arrived too and they sent immediately for the doctor and for the police.

Sergeant Peter Grant arrived from Kirkburton, quickly deciding that it was William Leather that he needed to speak to. He went in search of him, finally tracing him to the house of James Mosley, just behind the *Gardeners Arms*. The door was locked and no one answered his knock, but there was a

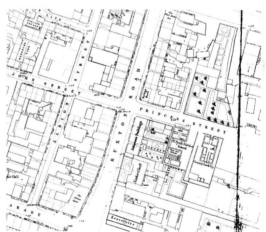

Map showing the County Lock-up, Huddersfield. Ordnance Survey

crack in the window blind and, on peering in through this, the sergeant could see two men sitting by the fire. He called out that it was the police at the door, but got no answer. When he saw Leather get up and go towards the back, the policeman shouted that if he didn't open the door he would break it down. At that, Leather unlocked the door and was immediately charged with cutting and wounding Lucy Thornton. Leather's reply was simply that:

If she had not begun first I should not have done what I did.

The officer then took Leather back to Lucy Thornton's house. By this time she was in bed, washed clean and under the care of Dr Dowse. She was still alive and had recovered sufficiently to recognise the man standing at the foot of her bed. Sergeant Grant turned to Leather and said:

You see the state this woman is in and I charge you with having committed those injuries upon her.

He said nothing, but Lucy muttered, 'Bill Leather has done it.' She managed to say that on the morning after the attack, having been left on the floor all night, she had asked Bill as he was leaving to tell the neighbours. He replied, 'You can tell the neighbours soon enough yourself.'

Leather was then taken to the lock-up at Kirkburton and his shirt examined. On the right sleeve was some blood and also on the front. As Leather insisted that Lucy had started the fight, the sergeant examined him but could not find any wounds or marks of injury. He was supplied with a clean shirt and trousers and taken to the county lock-up at Huddersfield.

At Huddersfield, the Superintendent, Thomas Heaton saw Leather in his cell, telling him that Lucy Thornton was very ill and in a dangerous state. Leather replied:

Well, I shouldn't have touched her if she had not struck me with a poker. I went into the house about half past nine and sat myself down to warm me. She came at me with the poker and I struck her with my fists.

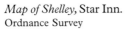
Map of Shelley, Star Inn.
Ordnance Survey

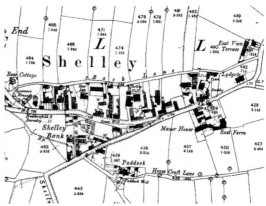

This did not agree with the publican's statement, which was that Leather had not left his inn until at least midnight. The superintendent also looked for signs of injury on Leather but found none.

The doctor, John Dowse of Skelmanthorpe, knew Lucy well having treated her for 'bilious attacks and dyspepsia' but he was very much shocked when he was called in to see her on the Tuesday. He found her in an exhausted state, with wounds on her forearm and face, from loss of blood. He ordered stimulants of beef tea to be given and treated the wounds. He went again the following morning, and again the next day. She had been sipping at the beef tea and he felt that she would eventually recover, but on the 24th he found her much worse, very weak and exhausted.

The local magistrates had initially remanded Leather into custody, awaiting Lucy's recovery so that she could appear in court, but as they met at the court on Thursday 25 January the police heard that Lucy had died that very morning. Leather was remanded again pending the coroner's inquest, which was heard at the *Star Inn*, Shelley by the deputy coroner, Thomas Taylor. Samuel Armitage was the foreman.

The evidence of the family and neighbours was heard, as well as that of James King, surgeon who performed the post-mortem examination. He described the inch and a half long wound across Lucy's forehead that had completely destroyed her right eye. She had bruises all over her body and damage at

Kirkburton church. The author

the base of her spine that had begun to turn gangrenous. She appeared to have been relatively healthy for her age, though she did have many gallstones that would probably have killed her in the end, but King stated that in his opinion the cause of death was exhaustion accelerated by the injuries that she had received. The injuries were such that it was impossible that they could have been produced by falls, but more likely to have been inflicted by hitting with a hard object or kicking with clogs tipped with iron, such as William Leather wore.

The Huddersfield magistrates had no difficulty in deciding that this was manslaughter and sent Leather to Leeds Assizes for trial.

At his trial in Leeds, Leather's defence was primarily that 'she started it'. The judge however, pointed out to the jury that it:

> *didn't matter if she was the first aggressor ... a person is only excusable for defending himself necessarily, but had no right to*

take it upon himself to punish a person as Leather must have punished the deceased.

The jury agreed that the verdict was manslaughter, the judge subsequently sentencing him to five years' imprisonment because, he said, Leather had:

committed an unmanly and cowardly outrage upon an old woman of seventy-two, who had done him no injury and for the crime he must undergo a severe punishment, which would have been heavier if the prisoner had not been an old man.

Lucy Thornton was buried in Kirkburton Parish Church 'by coroner's warrant' on 28 January 1866.

CHAPTER 21

Murder at Lockwood: Huddersfield 1888

It was not uncommon to hear of dreadful crimes happening in the slums of London, but the people of Huddersfield were shocked when it occurred on their doorstep.

Benjamin and Fanny Allerton left their home in Leeds sometime in the 1850s to secure work at Batley Carr. They took with them their family – William, Hannah, Elizabeth and Phoebe. They all found work in the mills and seemed settled in the area.

Elizabeth Allerton, who worked for M Oldroyd & Sons in Dewsbury, was just twenty-one when she married Joe Bailey in

Folly Hall Mills, Lockwood. The author

Batley Carr, fortunately just before their daughter, Fanny, was born. They too stayed near her parents, which she would have been glad about because within four years Joe had died.

In 1876 Elizabeth married Charles Bulmer, a groom or cab driver nine years her senior. Their eldest daughter, Sarah Ethel, was born a couple of years later, but the marriage proved somewhat volatile and the couple parted for over four years. Elizabeth and her daughter stayed with her mother in Batley, whilst Charles found work in Leeds, living in lodgings there.

The two kept in touch and by the end of 1881 decided to try again, this time moving to Lockwood in Huddersfield. Elizabeth found work in the local mills at Folly Hall, whilst Charles continued his work as a cab driver. All seemed settled for a number of years and the family expanded to include three more daughters.

Some time in 1887, Charles had an accident that, although he wasn't badly hurt, seems to have affected his attitude to life. He began drinking.

In November 1887 Elizabeth went to court to ask that he be bound over to keep the peace towards her. The couple had run up a number of debts and, in order to pay them off, they had agreed to sell the best of their furniture. Elizabeth had returned home from work to find Charles in the street, singing his head off. She took him home, where he gave her 18lb of beef and £2.10s (£2.50), which was all that was left of the money. In the ensuing argument, he took up the poker and threatened to kill her with it, driving her out of the house. Two witnesses came forward to support Elizabeth's tale of woe and Charles expressed his sorrow over his loss of temper, saying that he only earned £1 per week but tried his best to support his family on this. The court bound him over in the sum of £10 to keep the peace for six months.

Just six months later, the pair were back in court, Elizabeth making similar charges. This time, after finding him drinking in a pub and getting him home, she asked for some money to buy food. He offered ten shillings (50p) but when she asked for 'the remainder', he took some more change out of his pocket to count it. In a fit of temper, she knocked it out of his hand, whereupon he knocked her down and kicked her. Again he threatened her saying he would 'make her so she would not go to the police office or anywhere else telling tales'. Again, he was bound over for six months, though when Elizabeth said that she dare not live with him, the members of the Bench - the Mayor, Alderman Brooke, J Crosland, C E Freeman and J Lowenthal (who had all been present at the previous case) told her:

> ... *they could not help thinking that she was a little to blame for the manner in which she behaved on Saturday night. In future, she ought to be more circumspect in her conduct and not give her husband any provocation.*

Just four months later she and Charles argued again. This time they decided to separate again and he moved out of the house to go and lodge with the Gibson family on St Stephen's Road, Lockwood.

On Monday 10 September Elizabeth went to visit her friend and neighbour, Elizabeth Bailey, complaining to her about the ill-treatment she had received from her husband and commenting that the magistrates refused to believe how afraid she was because she had no bruises, though, she said 'the first mark that she ever had to show would be the last, for he would do for her'.

Just after nine o'clock Elizabeth Bulmer set off home, accompanied by her friend for part of the way. The two women stopped to speak to William Crabb, who was engaged to Elizabeth's daughter. As they stood there Mrs Bailey saw Charles Bulmer approaching and immediately ran away since he had previously threatened her. Bulmer followed her a short way, then turned off into the *Star Inn*. A little later, the Bulmers were seen together and they seemed to be arguing; he wanted his clothes and she was refusing to let him into the house unless a policeman accompanied him. Bulmer appears to have agreed to fetch one and turned away, but another neighbour, Eliza Buckley, saw him turn back and follow his wife into the narrow passage that led through to their house. Eliza was so worried she ran to fetch the police fearing what

Star Inn, *Lockwood.* The author

Bulmer would do. Though PC Walters went to the house, all seemed quiet.

In the meantime, Bulmer went away from the house and accosted Sergeant Callaghan, asking for help in obtaining his clothes from the house. The sergeant recommended that Bulmer go with a civilian but agreed to return to Lockwood with him, where the policeman waited outside the passageway until Bulmer returned and told him that everyone was asleep and he would wait until morning. Callaghan agreed that this was the best course and watched Bulmer go off towards the *Dusty Miller* inn. He afterwards commented that Bulmer seemed 'perfectly cool and composed, but his breath smelt of drink'. Just before 10 pm he and PC Simpson returned to the Bulmer's house, finding a bundle of clothes outside but all was quiet.

A little later, the eldest daughter, Ethel, woke up and heard her father threatening her mother, though she didn't hear the woman speak at all. The girl screamed which seems to have caused Bulmer to run out of the house, banging the door behind him. The neighbours who lived in the front of the back-to-back terrace house also heard screaming and Bulmer shouting.

Around ten o'clock Elizabeth Bailey decided to check that Mrs Bulmer had reached home safely. She found the door unfastened and walked in. Mrs Bulmer was lying on the floor in a pool of blood.

Horrified, she ran out to give the alarm, finding PCs Walters and Simpson still in the vicinity. They returned with her and Walters ran for Dr McGregor, who lived close by, but it was already too late. Elizabeth Bulmer was dead, though the body was still warm and blood was flowing from the gash across her throat, which had almost severed her head. Underneath her body they found a thimble, a man's felt hat and the front door key.

Charles Bulmer seems to have visited a neighbour, John Hartley, walking through to the kitchen and calmly washing his hands, telling the Hartley children (Laura Jane and John junior) that 'he had done for his wife for ever and that he would swing for her'. He gave the young lad a leather case containing two white handled razors and asked him to wash the blood off and take care of them. He then picked up a hat from the clothes horse and went out. Mrs Hartley immediately sent out, found PC Simpson and gave him the razors.

Charles Bulmer gave himself up to the police later that night, walking into the police office in Huddersfield where he was charged with murder.

An inquest was held by W Barstow, the coroner, in the *Victoria Hotel*, Lockwood Road before a jury consisting of: G H Heppleston (foreman); J H Taylor, C Rothery, Thomas Bagshaw, John Davis, assistant overseer for Huddersfield, Jonas Horsfall, John Horsfall, James Liddington, D Brown, W Wright, Law Hargreaves, Alfred Rhodes and Walter Wigglesworth.

Fanny Bailey identified her mother, stating that she had lived for the past year in Earlsheaton with her uncle William, but prior to that she had lived with her mother, stepfather and half sisters.

Elizabeth Bailey (no relation) described the events of the previous night, confirming that she had frequently had to give

Victoria Hotel, *Lockwood.*

refuge to Mrs Bulmer and had often heard Charles making threats against his wife. Bulmer had become more violent because his wife had asked the court for help, though he was also of a jealous disposition too. Mrs Bailey was indignant when the jury implied that the husband had grounds for suspicion. 'Why, there wasn't a decenter woman!' she exclaimed.

As the four little girls lay in bed, Ethel, aged just eleven, told the court how she heard her father shouting, 'If I draw my knife, you b****, where will you be then?' and later, 'If you don't give up talking, I'll kill you,' though Ethel insisted that she never heard her mother say a word. She confirmed that the razors in the leather case belonged to her father.

Mary Jane Ogden, who lived with her husband, Thomas and their children in the house adjoining the Bulmers' house, distinctly heard a scream at about five minutes to ten. She was confident it was a woman's scream, not a child's. She knocked hard on the wall and shouted out but Bulmer had already left. She described him as an 'idle, drunken villain,' but Mrs Bulmer 'worked every day'.

John Gibson explained that Bulmer had gone to lodge with him in early September and on the night in question he saw Bulmer coming from Folly Hall at around twenty-five to ten. The man stopped to talk to him, saying that he had gone to collect some clothes but the family were all asleep so he didn't disturb them. Bulmer was without a hat, but walking very fast. He told Gibson then that he had cut his wife's throat so was going to wash his hands and give himself up. Gibson did not believe that he had really killed his wife.

Dr McGregor described finding the body and confirmed that death would have been instant at the time of the first gash to the throat. The carotid and other arteries were severed and Mrs Bulmer had had no time to offer any resistance.

The jury decided they had heard sufficient to make a decision, bringing in a verdict of wilful murder and committing Bulmer to Leeds for trial.

The local paper gave a full description of the prisoner, saying that he wore:

> *… a black coat and waistcoat, is a tall man of powerful build and healthy appearance and does not look his age. He has by no means a cruel face, except, perhaps, some determined hardness about the mouth, which is clean shaved.*

It goes on to describe his 'thick, dark hair' and 'blue eyes, straight nose, brown whiskers … and a beard after the Yankee style'. His demeanour was described as calm 'without showing either excitement or emotion'.

On 13 December Bulmer appeared before Baron Pollock at Leeds Town Hall. Mr Harold Thomas prosecuted for the Crown and Mr Scout Fox was for the defence. The evidence was sifted through once more, Mr Thomas stressing that Elizabeth Bulmer had been an upright citizen and hard working millhand, so the blame for the events did not lie with her.

Joe Lewis, a warehouseman, said he had known Bulmer for over four years and had met him on the night of the murder at about twenty past ten. They had gone into the *Greyhouse Inn* and had a beer, when Bulmer had confessed to the murder.

Lewis was afraid that he would be implicated in the matter, but eventually agreed to go back to Bulmer's house to see what had happened. On his return he had informed Bulmer that his wife was dead. Bulmer merely replied, 'I'm glad she is, I would rather she should be dead than linger. Get another glass.' Lewis refused to buy any more beer. Together they then walked towards the police office, all the while Bulmer talking about what he had done. Bulmer went into the police station on his own and Lewis went home.

The defence made much of the fact that Bulmer was not drunk before the events described and that everyone, including his daughter, had stated that he was a kind man and good father until he drank. Bulmer had no motive for killing his wife – it was an unreasonable crime, and therefore the perpetrator was not 'in possession of his understanding'. Bulmer had said that he had simply reached for his razor, his wife had pulled his arm down and 'in a moment, with the razor in his hand, the deed was done'. But when he entered the house he had no intention of killing his wife.

The Cemetery, Dewsbury.

The judge summed up, describing to the jury the evidence needed to use insanity as a defence (which he did not think was provided in this case), commenting on the level of drink consumed (or not) by the prisoner and reminding them that 'drink was no excuse for crime'.

The jury retired to consider their verdict, but came back a couple of hours later to ask whether 'in the event of one person killing another without premeditation, the crime would be one of murder or manslaughter?'

The judge explained that if a person killed another without premeditation, and there was no sufficient cause such as a fight or sudden emergency that would reduce the crime to manslaughter, then it would be murder. Eventually the jury agreed on a verdict of murder, but with a recommendation for mercy. The hanging was deferred until the outcome of the recommendation could be decided, but on New Year's Day 1889 Charles Bulmer was hanged for the murder of his wife.

An editorial in the *Huddersfield Examiner* commented that Bulmer was a decent man, when not in drink, and that 'total abstinence [from drink] is the right course for many, especially those who know the effect it has on them'.

Elizabeth Bulmer was buried in Dewsbury Cemetery near her first husband. The streets around Lockwood were lined with people seeing the coffin off on its journey. Wreaths were sent from the workers and firm of F Eastwood & Co where Elizabeth had worked. More people lined the streets in Dewsbury and Batley Carr as the funeral procession arrived at the cemetery and her future son-in-law, William Crabb, was one of the coffin bearers.

CHAPTER 22

An Atrocious Case of Murder: Knaresborough 1841

The *Leeds Mercury* described this murder as 'one of the most atrocious, cool and deliberate murders ever committed'.

In the Market Place at Knaresborough, Joseph Cocker ran the *Old White Hart* inn. Everyone agreed that 'a more quiet, harmless and inoffensive man it is universally acknowledged never existed'. He lived alone, aged fifty-six, a widower with no children, no housekeeper and no servants. On 17 June, a group of three young men came into his beer house, drinking and chatting happily until Mr Inchbold, the employer of one of them, decided to stop off to have one last drink. The three young men left.

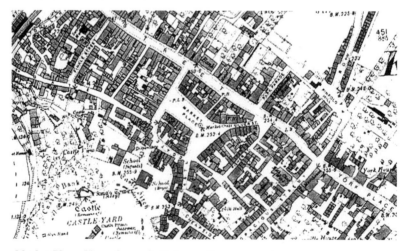

Market Place, Knaresborough. Ordnance Survey

The following night, Cocker's next-door neighbour, Mary Snow, was woken up by some strange noises, 'most piteous cries, as if someone was beating an animal'. She listened carefully and decided they were coming from the pub next door, which backed onto a shared yard. Creeping out of her house she peered in through her neighbour's window where she saw three young men, one of whom was holding a candle, giving her a clear view of the scene. Mrs Snow courageously dashed round to the front door and tried to open it but it was fastened. Knocking on the door, she cried out, 'Are they murdering you?' No one answered so she ran home to waken her husband. As soon as the coast was clear, the men rushed out of the front door. Mrs Snow returned, went in and found Joseph Cocker leaning against the chimney breast, crying for help. She went back to her own house to tell her husband, Charles, to hurry up, then returned next door. There she found that the young men had returned. This time, Cocker was laid on the floor, two of the men standing over him and one knelt beside him. Mr Snow rushed off for his pistol, but this time the three men left and did not return. He chased them up Synagogue Lane but lost them there, and went instead for the police, who returned with him to the inn.

Cocker was still alive but, despite sending for the local surgeon, Thomas Beaumont, the landlord died within a few minutes. The police then set off around Knaresborough to try to find the perpetrators, accurately described by Mrs Snow. Within an hour, all three had been arrested. John Burlinson, aged twenty-four, and Charles Gill, twenty, were both spattered with blood about the face and hands. Henry Nuttall, twenty-two, was less so, a fact which became important at the trial.

They confessed that the crime had been premeditated, intending to commit the deed on the previous night but Mr Inchbold interrupted them. They had hung on in the pub, drinking until late and then attacked the landlord with a hammer. Burlinson had struck the first blow, but had been disturbed by Mrs Snow. They had each run in different directions, but met up on the High Bridge before returning to finish the deed and complete the robbery. At this point the

High Bridge, Knaresborough. The author

prisoners began to differ in their story as to who had struck the fatal blows. Burlinson said at that time that Nuttall had struck the first blow, though he later changed this, and that Gill had later taken the hammer and struck Mr Cocker as he had sat near the fireplace. Nuttall said he had not taken part in any of the violence, that he had run away and the others had followed him. Gill, too, denied taking any part in the violence.

The coroner's inquest, held before John Wood, found Burlinson guilty of murder and the other two guilty of aiding and abetting him. All were sent to York for trial.

On Monday 19 July the 'court was crowded to suffocation at an early hour and a considerable portion of the auditory was composed of the inhabitants of Knaresborough' (*Leeds Mercury*).

The judge, Justice Wightman, informed the jury that there were three charges to be considered: Burlinson was the murderer, Gill and Nuttall aiding and abetting; or Gill was the murderer, Burlinson and Nuttall accessories; or all three were the principals.

The *Leeds Mercury* said that the prisoners were threadmakers 'of respectable appearance'. Burlinson was described as having 'the lower part of his head very heavy and forehead deficient. His whole expression of countenance indicative of a low order of intelligence.'

Gill was small with nothing 'in his face to indicate the cruelty of disposition which the evidence proved him to possess', whilst Nuttall seemed to be 'deeply moved', spending most of the trial apparently muttering prayers to himself.

Mr Knowles and Mr Martin prosecuted, Mr Wilkins defended Nuttall and Mr Newton defended Burlinson and Gill.

Joseph Dixon, Knaresborough's constable, described how he, his assistants and some 'respectable inhabitants' searched the town for the murderers. He found Gill near the riverside and took him to the courthouse. Next they went to Nuttall's father's house but the young man had not returned home. Later they found him on Bond End and he too was taken to the courthouse. John Burlinson was later found just twenty yards from Cocker's inn.

The Courthouse, Knaresborough. The author

Another police officer, David Vickerman, described the blood on the prisoners' clothes. Neither Burlinson nor Gill offered any explanation for this, but Nuttall said he had had a nosebleed which was why he had blood on his waistcoat and trousers.

The surgeon described severe wounds to the murdered man's head – a three-inch deep wound on the right and wounds to both cheeks. Both ears had been almost split from his head by the force of the various blows. Five other wounds were also found and the skull was fractured beneath each wound. The wound that killed him, on the right part of his head, was 'inflicted by some pointed instrument' according to the surgeon, possibly by the point of a hammer or poker, though Mr Beaumont felt these were both too large.

According to Burlinson, all three men knew what they were going to do and all were willing. The weapon belonged to Henry Nuttall – it was a long hammer with a square face. The weapon had been thrown in the river by Nuttall when they all met together at High Bridge after the event. Though Burlinson agreed that he had struck the first blow, he insisted that Gill had struck Joseph Cocker four or five times.

William Inchbold was able to confirm the ownership of the hammer. Inchbold was a tallow chandler in Knaresborough and Henry Nuttall had worked, on and off, for him. Inchbold had owned a cooper's adze that was about a foot long with a hole in the middle. At one end it was shaped like a hammer, at the other it was flat. It was seldom used but he had not seen it for the past five or six weeks. He also confirmed that he had seen Burlinson and Nuttall in Cocker's inn on 17 June and that the men had left soon after Inchbold had arrived.

Nuttall insisted that he was innocent. He acknowledged that he had been at Cocker's but said he went out into the yard to relieve himself and was not there when the blows were actually struck. He followed the others when they ran away and also when they went back, when he saw Gill strike Cocker a number of times with the hammer.

The defence took the line that the violence was merely the result of a scuffle that had broken out when Cocker had refused to serve any more beer and that the charge should have been manslaughter. Mr Wilkins, on behalf of Nuttall,

Market Cross, Knaresborough. The author

pointed out that none of the evidence pointed to his having struck any blow and that therefore Nuttall was entitled to be acquitted. The judge, in his summing up, pointed out to the jury that they must not take account of any one statement of the prisoners but look at the whole of the evidence presented but as regards Nuttall 'if he were present with the others for one common purpose, and aiding and assisting, he would be equally guilty with the man whose hand had struck the blow'.

Not surprisingly, the jury quickly returned a verdict of guilty of wilful murder against all three.

On Saturday 7 August, four ministers of the church – Rev W Flower, Rev J Shackley, Rev Thomas Richardson, and a Wesleyan minister, Rev J Rattenbury - accompanied the three men to the scaffold. All three prisoners had been very penitent prior to their execution but though Burlinson and Nuttall were able to walk unaided, Gill had become so ill that he needed support, though he managed to 'stand firm' on the scaffold itself, before the three were 'launched into eternity'. Many of the crowd watching were their friends and neighbours from Knaresborough.

CHAPTER 23

A Strange Suicide: Leeds
1847

Joseph Bolland, aged nineteen and Maria Wilson, seventeen, both lived in Lincoln Field Place, Newtown, Leeds. They were sweethearts, looking forward to their future but both were out of work.

On a Wednesday morning in April they set off from their homes and visited a number of friends and relatives, having breakfast with one family, tea with another and spent the evening having a party with their young friends. All this because they had decided to set off 'on the tramp' to find work. First they were going to Harrogate, then they also mentioned they'd been offered work in France, though no one could find out what sort of work or how they were going to get there. They set off that evening, wishing a cheery goodbye to everyone.

Next morning their bodies were dragged from the river, at Knostrop, 'bound together by handkerchiefs which had previously been the reciprocal tokens of affection'. The inquest was held on Thursday morning at the courthouse, before John Blackburn.

Maria's sister, Martha, who lived at Mabgate Green in Leeds told the court that about five months ago Maria had gone to live at the Bolland's house. She had been 'walking out' with Joseph for about three years and had been working at the flax mill of Hives and Atkinson in Banks Mill, East Street, Leeds but about three weeks ago had lost her job. Joseph had been out of work for many months.

Maria and Joseph had visited Martha on Wednesday 7 April, getting a wash and having coffee with her. The girl had bought some print cloth to make herself an apron but offered to give it to Martha so that a little dress could be made for her baby. Maria had kissed the baby and said 'goodbye' to it, saying she would never see it alive again, but Martha did not seem to question this. The young couple told her they were going off to Harrogate so perhaps she assumed that Maria was simply being dramatic or gloomy. Martha told the court that Maria was 'not in the family way that I'm aware of'.

Joseph's mother explained that Maria had come to live with them since she was 'without a mother'. She generally got up around 6.30 am, lit the fire and went out to work around seven. Since losing her job three weeks previously she was often 'low spirited' and had once commented that she might drown herself.

Maria's aunt, Harriet Hellowell, told how the young couple had visited her on Wednesday afternoon. The two women had drunk coffee, but Joseph had drunk beer. Maria had told her aunt that they were going to be married on Whit Monday, but she had advised waiting a couple of years. Joseph had replied, 'The sooner we get married, the better.' Around five o'clock she saw them go off from her house in Brussel Street, down Bridge Street. Maria had no bonnet on, but was wearing a handkerchief.

Mary Dinsdale was a friend of the lovers, meeting them in Duke Street at seven o'clock. Both seemed cheerful and all three went to Thomas Wilson's in Sykes Row, where they stayed drinking for over an hour. Maria began talking about going to France and saying they 'would never see her again'. When asked where the money would come from Joseph replied that they had as much as they needed. They told the company that they were going to set off between nine and ten that night, going 'on the water' which was taken to mean a canal flyboat which went every evening up to Goole and thence to Hull. When Joseph and Maria left, the girl seemed depressed, though Joseph did not. Earlier in the week Mary and Maria had met up and chatted, Maria saying that she felt that the Bollands 'could not do with her' because she no longer had a job.

Joseph's friend, Thomas Wilson, junior, described how the two of them had drunk a pint of ale at Wilson's home where they had discussed the proposed trip to France. Joseph had told him the fare was already paid and they'd have plenty to eat and drink where they were going, but refused to say the name of their prospective employer. The group had walked along the waterside for a while, then returned to the Wilson's home, where Bolland paid for another pint. They talked about marriage, Joseph saying they would probably be married in Hull, then had some supper of bread and sausages. The atmosphere was cheerful and the lads sang *I am a Rover* together. Both were a little the worse for drink by the end of the evening.

John Imeson confirmed the general conversation. Bolland had told him they had 'pledged' some trousers and a waistcoat for three shillings and six pence, though only six pence was left, all the rest having been spent on food and drink. They were leaving Leeds, he said at half past ten to catch an early morning flyboat to Hull. When Imeson left, around nine at night, Bolland shook hands and 'said he would not see me any more'.

Though none of their friends worried over the young couple's disappearance, when they did not return home that night, the Bolland family became concerned. PC Marsden began searching for them in the morning and by 8.15 am had found their bodies in the river near a carpet factory. They were in each other's arms, tied together with two handkerchiefs. It was noted that the handkerchiefs were both tied at Joseph's back. A jacket, cap and the girl's slip were found nearby on the riverbank.

The coroner said it was the most remarkable case he had ever come across. That they had destroyed themselves was undisputed but what the jury had to decide was whether they were insane or not at the time they committed 'self-destruction'. Their actions seemed to be inconsistent with any intention to destroy themselves and to his mind 'negated any notion of their being insane'.

The verdict of the jury agreed with him. They had 'destroyed themselves' and were at the time in a sane state of mind.

CHAPTER 24

Manslaughter at Ferrybridge: Pontefract
1837

The Richardson family were well known around the Ferrybridge area. In 1802 Rylah Richardson married Catherine Lowther at St Giles' church, Pontefract, thereby becoming stepfather to her illegitimate son, Robert, who was then four years old.

The pair lived somewhat unhappily ever after. Robert's relationship with Rylah was never very good and many times Rylah had ordered him out of the house. Eventually he declared he would never have him back again. Robert, who had become a butcher and beer seller, like his stepfather, moved away to Knottingley, along with his wife Mary, their son James and four daughters, Catherine, Anne, Elizabeth and Mary.

Catherine continued to abuse her husband, complaining generally but most especially about his treatment of her son. On Sunday 24 November, Rylah was so fed up with her nagging that he got more than a little the worse for drink, which was not unusual, and took himself off to bed. Catherine immediately sent for her son to come to the house. Robert arrived before tea and stayed with his mother for the rest of the afternoon. Also in the kitchen were the two lodgers, John Hobson and his son James. When Rylah came downstairs, he ordered Robert out of the house, picking up a poker and threatening him with it. Robert's reply was to hit his stepfather, knocking him back into the armchair. He grabbed his stepfather by the hair and banged his head against the back of the chair a number of times. Rylah got up, wrenched open the door and said he was going for the constable. 'I'll see whether I can have peace in my own house or not,' he said.

Robert immediately replied, 'Aye, damn thee, I'll give thee something to fetch him for.'

Robert was determined to stop him, hitting Rylah with such force that the old man fell across the threshold of the door. But Lowther wasn't finished. He dragged Rylah back into the room, grasping his stepfather by the hair and proceeded to

St Giles' Church, Pontefract. The author

beat his head repeatedly on the stone flags of the kitchen floor. John Hobson, who had known Rylah for over seventy years, decided it was now time to intervene, pushed Robert away and tried to lift Rylah. Lowther rushed to the door and bolted it, determined to keep the neighbours out, but the multitude outside, led by Ann Sawyer, their next-door neighbour who had heard the commotion, were equally determined to enter the house. The inmates, realising that the door would break, undid the bolts and let them in. Mr Laidman, the constable from Ferrybridge was sent for and Rylah was placed on a chair, but died within minutes.

Catherine Richardson tried to claim that her husband had died 'in a fit of passion' but no one believed her. Both she and her son were arrested, appearing before the coroner, M Pearson, the following Monday. Unfortunately, no one could decide what to charge her with so she was released, though the coroner commented that she was worse than her son and was the principal cause of her husband's death. On Tuesday, Lowther was taken to York for trial. Catherine's only concern was her son and the punishment he was likely to receive.

Rylah was buried in St Andrew's churchyard, Ferry Fryston (Ferrybridge) on the following day, escorted by a large crowd.

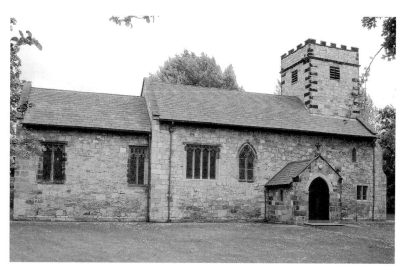

St Andrew's Church. The author

Once the funeral had taken place, that same crowd turned on the widow, hanging and burning her effigy in front of her own door and eventually the police had to come to her rescue. She was not only hounded out of Ferry Fryston but could find no refuge with her daughter-in-law in Knottingley either. No villages in the area would let her stay in peace and she eventually moved away.

In March, Lowther came before Mr Justice Coleridge in York. Sergeant Atcherley and Mr Reed presented the case for the prosecution. The surgeon described the bruising on Rylah's head and brain, confirming that it was this 'external violence' which had caused death. The neighbours repeated the evidence they had given to the coroner. In his defence, Sir G Lewin pointed out that the man had been killed, not in a premeditated way, but in 'heated blood and after considerable provocation' therefore it was not murder. The jury agreed and found Lowther guilty of manslaughter. Judge Coleridge found no fault with this verdict but pointed out that no one should think they could 'take away human life and get away with it'. He went on to comment on the state of the calendar, which seemed to be full of similar events so that he felt that in the area 'little value was set upon life. The state of society, amongst the lower orders, more resembled an uncivilized and barbarian country than Christian England.' He then sentenced Lowther to transportation for life. Lowther spent almost a year on the hulk *Fortitude* in Chatham before being transferred to the transport ship *Barossa* which sailed for New South Wales, Australia in August 1839, arriving in December.

CHAPTER 25

The Great Mail Robbery: Rotherham
1791

Spence Broughton seemed to have everything to live for. He was born in 1744 in Horbling, Lincolnshire, the son of John and Anne Broughton, a reasonably well-off farming family. In 1770 he married Frances Graves at Folkingham, Lincolnshire and they had at least two children – Spence, born in 1771 and Frances born in 1777. Frances was a wealthy young woman and they lived in style, until Spence took up with another woman. By the time Frances obtained a separation from him, he had already squandered over £1,500.

An eighteenth-century mail coach. British Postal Museum and Archive

John Oxley was born at Wentworth and found employment in the stables at Wentworth House. At that time Royal Mail coaches delivered mail only to the main towns such as Sheffield and Rotherham, from where it had to be collected by recipients. Putting his riding skills to good use Oxley had the job of carrying the letterbag between Rotherham and Wentworth, so he knew the postal system well.

The two men got to know each other, probably at the cock fights which they frequented. Somehow they also came into contact with John Close from Change Alley, Sheffield, though he also had a 'wife' in London and Thomas Shaw, a receiver, fence and would-be mastermind. Shaw thought up the idea of robbing the Avebury mail coach, which he and Broughton put into effect on 28 May 1790 but they found nothing in it and by that job Shaw, who provided the money, lost £14. Undeterred, Shaw went to Cambridge to learn their system and work out the best means of robbing it. He returned and put together a plan with Broughton and Oxley, which they executed on 19 June. This time they found Bank of England notes amounting to £400, Stamford Bank notes amounting to £200 or £300 plus a variety of other bills amounting in all to around £10,000, though they could not use all of it – this was a time when different banks issued their own notes and personalised cheques were not produced. Instead bills of exchange were used. These are notes which require the addressee to pay the amount stated at a set time to the bearer or a specified person. However, Shaw had worked in the insurance industry and had apparently found out how to 'extract' the writing using spirit of salts. Afterwards, he would say that although he knew the theory he had never actually done the deed, Oxley being the one who had made changes to bills cashed.

After this success, further plans were made to rob other mail coaches. Meeting together at Shaw's house in Prospect Place, St George's Field the men agreed on a plan of action. As neither Broughton nor Oxley had any money, Shaw provided Broughton with funds for a journey north. They set off in the Nottingham coach and spent the night in Nottingham, intending to travel on to Chesterfield by coach, but the coach was full so, the two men had to walk and beg lifts where they could. From Chesterfield they walked out on the Rotherham road and saw the mail coach heading towards Sheffield. They decided they would do better to wait for its return, which they did in fields near the main road.

Broughton produced an old smock and hat. Taking the gate to the field off its hinges he told Oxley to wait and he would lead the coach in. Soon after Oxley heard a cart and then Broughton saying that he had got it and secured the post boy. The mails were soon removed and the two set off on foot to Mansfield. Once there Broughton pretended that he was sick and could not go any further, recommending Oxley to go on without him and try to cash a bill for £123 which was drawn by Monsieur Virgelle, a merchant from France, on the house of Minnet & Fector, merchants in London, payable to Joseph Walker of Rotherham.

Oxley did just that, giving the bill to Charles Lisk (or Leask), a porter at the Inner Temple who obtained cash for it. Later Broughton arrived in London seeking Oxley. On being told that he was in Leicester, watching some cock fighting, he went to Leicester himself to ensure he got his share of the booty.

On Monday 16 October 1791 a man and woman called at a silversmith's shop in Cheapside, London. They bought a ring for ten shillings and sixpence (53p) and asked the owner, Mr Metham, to change a £10 bill for it. Mr Metham declined so then the couple also bought a cream jug for £1 11s 6d (£1.58). This brought the total to £2 2s (£2.10) after which the silversmith agreed the deal, giving them change for the Stamford Bank note. The same couple then went into a haberdashery shop, bought some silk, and also went into Mr Mosley's grocers shop on the same street. At each shop they changed a bank note which later proved to have come from the Cambridge mail robbery.

Two days later a young man employed by Mr Metham spotted the man who had given his employer the stolen note. The boy ran after him, following him over Blackfriar's bridge, along Fleet Street, through Smithfield and to a pub in Clerkenwell. He waited outside until he saw a police officer, told him the tale and they went into the pub, where the man was dining with the landlord and lady. The policeman promptly arrested the man and took him before magistrate, Sampson Wright. There the man said his name was John Oxley and he had been given the bills by Thomas Shaw.

Two Bow Street Runners were sent off to Shaw's house. He wasn't there but as the runners were searching the house for him, another man knocked on the door. As soon as he realised there were Runners in the house, he scarpered, with the officers in hot pursuit. They caught up with him at the *Dog and Duck* in St George's Fields. The man turned out to be Broughton and was found with stolen bills on him.

It did not take long for Shaw to decide to turn King's Evidence, insisting that he had really had little to do with the events, merely received the bills, whereas Broughton and Oxley both insisted that it was Shaw who had masterminded the whole thing. Broughton was committed to Newgate, Shaw to Tothill Fields and Oxley to Clerkenwell prison. Later Broughton was transferred to York to stand trial for the Rotherham robbery, as this case seemed to have the most evidence against him.

In November advertisements appeared in a number of newspapers asking for information, and offering a reward, for the capture of John Oxley, who was described as aged twenty-five, 5 feet 10 inches tall, pale faced and rather pitted with small pox, with his nose turned to the right. He was said to be wearing a dark green coat, striped waistcoat and corduroy breeches. The reward was originally £50 but rose to £200,

York prison buildings. The author

offered by the Postmaster General. It appears that the window of the Clerkenwell prison was opened, some workmen had accidentally left a ladder against a wall near his cell and somehow Oxley had escaped, got up on the roof then run along until he could get down from the roofs of houses nearby. One of the gaolers raised the alarm eventually but by the time the constables arrived, Oxley was nowhere in sight. Later he appears to have approached a number of friends, some of whom must have provided him with fresh clothes and money. A comment appeared in the *General Evening Post* in February 1792 to the effect that Oxley had escaped out of the country with the help of the Folkestone smugglers and was gone to America. How they got that information was not stated.

The turnkey, Roberts, and a householder, Mary Smith of Portpool Lane, were quickly brought before Nicholas Bond, magistrate. Mary Smith agreed that she had known Oxley for some months but denied that he had come to her house. His prison irons were found near her house and she was eventually indicted for 'receiving, harbouring, aiding and encouring' him to escape. No further evidence was forthcoming and the courts had to bring in a verdict of 'not guilty'.

In York, Broughton appeared before Justice Buller, charged with the robbery of the Rotherham mail. Witnesses were brought to prove the journey of Broughton and Oxley up to Rotherham, the post boy, George Leasley, stating that it was, in fact, Oxley who had stopped the cart, tied the boy up and actually robbed him of the mails. Other witnesses confirmed the presence of Broughton at Mansfield and at Leicester with Oxley. Townsend, a Bow Street Runner, confirmed Broughton's arrest, stating that on searching his house in London, they'd found many bills and notes, though most of these seemed to relate to the Cambridge robbery. They also found a suit with buttons of pure gold. These had the impression of the crest and motto of the Prince Regent, later George IV.

The jury brought in a verdict of guilty. On pronouncing his sentence, the judge specified that it was not enough that Broughton should hang. He must be made an example of, and his body should be taken from York to Attercliffe Common, to hang in chains.

Much of the evidence against Broughton was provided by Thomas Shaw. On the scaffold, Broughton freely forgave everyone, except Shaw, whom he said should have been there with him, if not instead of himself.

After the hanging, Broughton's body was removed to Atterclife, where a large crowd watched as the soldiers hoisted the body on to the post. The landlord of the *Arrow* pub nearby did good business that day. He was also witness to another visit, about a month later, of a middle-aged woman who was supposed to have been Broughton's wife.

Early in 1793 a man was seen wandering around the Rotherham district. A few weeks later, in February, his body was discovered in a barn on Loxley moor, Sheffield. It appeared that he had died of cold and hunger, some bits of nibbled, raw turnips being found in his pocket. A man who said he had seen Oxley at Darnall, near Sheffield, a few weeks earlier said he thought the body was Oxley, since he was wearing the same clothes. The studs on his shirt-wrists were marked as 'DE' which were the initials of one of his gambling friends in London. The body was buried in an unmarked grave in Bradfield churchyard.

St Nicholas, Bradfield. The author

CHAPTER 26

A Quick Poisoning: Saddleworth 1850

Everyone felt sorry for William Ross. He was only nineteen, which seemed such a young age to be hanged.

In 1849 William had met and married Mary Bottomley, daughter of William and Betty Bottomley, from Ashton-under-Lyne. William was involved with the Chartist movement which was causing such trouble for the authorities, but nothing was ever proved against him.

The Bottomley family moved to Roughtown, Quick near Saddleworth, then in the West Riding of Yorkshire, in order to obtain work in the local mills there. In September of that year William and his new wife went to live with his in-laws, renting a room in their house and paying one shilling and sixpence rent ($7\frac{1}{2}$p).

In May 1850 William's sister, Jane, arrived in Roughtown, having also obtained work in one of the factories. However, it was not long before Mary and her mother began to argue, apparently over the state of the girl's clothes. William became very angry over this and insisted Jane go home to Ashton. Her brother went with her, staying overnight in Ashton and not returning home until the next morning. This led to considerable ill-feeling between the various members of the family. On one occasion William told the local constable that his mother-in-law and her son, John, had stolen some goods belonging to another lodger in the house. The pair were arrested and later appeared in the magistrates' court. The case was eventually thrown out, but only because William was no longer able to appear to confirm his accusation. Later it was to be suggested that it was William who had been stealing but this was never proved. On more than one occasion he and Mary were apparently heard arguing, during which William was supposedly heard to say to her that she was 'worth more dead than wick'. Mary belonged to two welfare clubs in the area and, on her death, more than £10 would be paid to her widower.

Two weeks later, on Tuesday 28 May, Mary became ill with sickness and diarrhoea. Her sister, Martha Buckley, came to visit and asked William to go for Dr Scholefield. He went out, reporting back that the doctor was out but his wife had promised to send him over as soon as possible. The doctor never arrived. On the Thursday Mary seemed a little better, sharing a breakfast with the family before they left for work. She and William were alone in the house until around ten o'clock, when he went out to the *George* pub in the village. There his drinking companions advised him to fetch the doctor as soon as possible. William arranged for Dr Halkyard to call. This doctor prescribed kaolin and opium, which Ross bought for his wife. Just before the doctor arrived, Ross moved his wife from the bed where she'd been ill to a different bed in the room nearby. Martha Buckley remained with her sister until Mary's death at two o'clock that afternoon.

William was immediately arrested but he quickly threw suspicion on his sister-in-law, telling the constable that she had given his wife some white powder, which she had said was cream of tartar in treacle. It was after this that Mary had become really ill and Martha was supposed to have said that she hoped she hadn't made any mistake in the powder. Ross believed that this was the cause of death and said he had heard her saying that she wished Mary was dead. Martha, and her husband, Philip, were soon arrested, but released after a short time without being charged.

Two weeks after the death of his daughter, William Bottomley moved from the house, during which time it was discovered that the mattress she had been lying on when she was initially ill was discoloured and a small hole was found. On being taken apart, a twist of paper containing arsenic was found. It was then that the local constable suddenly realised that he hadn't actually searched William Ross. On doing so, he found arsenic powder in the man's watch pocket. Ross then said that after Martha had given some of the poison to his wife, he had put the rest of the powder inside his watch fob. He also claimed that the Buckleys had given him a shilling to say nothing about the events, as it was simply a mistake on Martha's part. Ross later changed his mind about where the poison had come from, this time stating that he had bought it and given it to Martha for her to kill vermin in her house. It was later proved that he had, in fact, bought it in Ashton when he had escorted his sister there at the beginning of May. The post-mortem examination confirmed the presence of arsenic in the stomach and liver.

At his trial in York, Sergeant Wilkins for the defence pointed out that Ross had no motive to kill his wife since she was the sole breadwinner, then earning around ten shillings (50p). It was Martha who had had the opportunity of giving her sister arsenic. At the very least there was room for reasonable doubt that Ross had committed the deed. The jury disagreed and brought in a verdict of guilty. Ross vehemently denied this, and continued to do so. Justice Cresswell sentenced him to hang at York on 10 August, but this was remitted for one week to allow for further investigations and for a petition, raised by many of his neighbours and signed by over 2000 people, including the Mayor, to be sent to London for a pardon.

The three magistrates from Saddleworth, J Buckley, H Whitehead and T Robinson, were asked to go over the evidence again, meeting at the *White Hart* in Saddleworth and re-examining the witnesses. This time a rather different tale was told, as more witnesses were brought forward.

George Gill, a chemist in Ashton stated that ten days before Mary's death, a 'female' had come asking for arsenic. He refused to sell this to her as it would be illegal without a witness. She had then said she lived in Mossley and didn't have a witness but knew she could get it anyway. Gill pointed out Martha Buckley as the woman asking for arsenic. Jane Ross confirmed that Martha had asked William to 'save her the trouble' and fetch some arsenic. Ross had openly bought the arsenic in Ashton, with a witness to that effect, which was unusual behaviour if he intended to poison his wife. Ann Platt, who worked at Gressil Mill in Mossley confirmed that Martha had told her she'd obtained some 'mark'ry' or arsenic. She also said that when Martha had told her Mary was dead she had said, 'Our Mary's a damned bad 'un and he's no better', suggesting she was not the loving sister she had pretended to be. John Buckley JP and Henry Buckley, a retired police officer, agreed. John Bottomley and Martha Buckley were the principal witnesses against Ross but they were 'utterley unworthy of credit'.

At the trial it had been suggested that all the drawers in Ross's room had been locked, but Jane Worsnep came forward to refute this, saying that she had opened all but one when she'd been searching for something whilst looking after Mary. Moses Jackson also related that he had been at Dr Scholefield's and the servant girl had said that Ross had been there earlier but since the doctor was unavailable, they'd sent him on to Dr Halkyard, which is what Ross actually did do. Isaac Butterworth a chemist also stated that Ross had brought Mary to see him to get medicine for her, which was hardly the action of a man intent on murdering his wife.

The feeling in the village was that Ross was the victim of a conspiracy and at the very least the new evidence threw sufficient discredit on the previous witnesses that the case should be retried, if not dismissed. Neighbours said he was fond of his wife and seemed 'much affected by her death'. Throughout his stay in York Castle gaol, Ross maintained his innocence. No amount of coaxing from the Castle chaplain, Thomas Sutton, could persuade Ross to confess his guilt.

Sir George Grey, Secretary of State, refused to accept any doubt of Ross's guilt or the propriety of the verdict, stating that he could not 'interfere with the due course of the law'.

On Saturday 17 August, William Ross was escorted to the gallows and, watched by a crowd of three or four thousand people, 'the sufferings of this unfortunate young man in this vale of tears were for ever at an end' by Nathaniel Howard, the executioner.

However, most criminals confessed their guilt when faced with the hangman's noose. That Ross did not suggests that either he had convinced himself that he was innocent or possibly that he had told the truth. After his death, it is possible that Martha could have collected the £10 burial

Headline, Leeds Mercury, 1850.
Author's collection

EXECUTION OF WILLIAM ROSS,
FOR MURDER.

On Saturday last, at twelve o'clock, William Ross, the young man convicted at the York assizes of the murder of his wife at Roughtown, in the parish of Quick, near Ashton, was hanged at York Castle. The facts of this case, and the

money. Perhaps she was jealous of her sister or they had simply argued about something. It is something we will never know.

Numerous letters were written to the newspapers over this case. It was pointed out that the reinvestigation had not been in open court and that:

> ... *surely in such a case ... a more lengthened respite, at least, might have been granted and evidence publicly called for and heard. Instead of this, the friends of the prisoner appeal to Sir George Grey and the latter consults the judge who presided over the trial of the man and who summed up in favour of hanging him.* (Manchester Times)

Some people suggested that the final result was more because of Ross's Chartist involvement than his wife's death. One letter went on to suggest that there was:

> ... *something indecent in the hasty manner and mode with which it* [the evidence] *is examined and the prisoner hastened to execution.* (Manchester Times)

Ross was buried in the prison grounds.

CHAPTER 27

Savage Assault at Brayton: Selby 1870

J ohn Rawlinson was the eldest son of Thomas, a shoemaker and Hannah, from Sherburn. He seems to have had a good education and by the time he was twenty-four had moved to Hambleton near Selby where he was appointed schoolmaster. His wife, Mary, who was born and bred in Hambleton, helped out in the school when she wasn't looking after their growing family of five girls and one boy. They seem to have been quite settled, staying at the schoolhouse for at least a dozen years.

William James Nappey (also known as Nappy, Napley, Napier) was a rather different type. He was a farm labourer from the nearby village of Newland. In 1864 he had married

Red Lion Inn, *Hambleton.* The author

New courthouse, Selby. The author

Sarah Palframan, the eldest daughter of a local farmer and thirteen years William's senior. They quickly began a family, a son and two daughters.

Fate brought the two men together on Thursday 20 May 1870. On that night, Rawlinson decided to visit the *Red Lion* in Hambleton with two of his friends, Mr Brown and Mr Stott. They stayed drinking until late, though none was actually drunk, unlike Nappey who had imbibed rather too much. Outside he started throwing stones in their general direction and Rawlinson called out that he was a fool to do so in the dark. Without warning, Nappey flung himself at Rawlinson and in the midst of the scuffle, drew a knife, stabbing at his adversary and inflicting wounds to his shoulder and head. The other men dragged him off and handed him over to the constable.

He appeared first before the magistrates at Selby Court House where his excuse was that he thought the three men were going to kill him and he was frightened for his life. The bench were not impressed and sent him off to Leeds for trial.

Nappey repeated his story to Judge Brett on 13 August at Leeds Town Hall. It did not take the jury long to decide that Nappey was guilty of 'unlawfully and maliciously wounding with a knife...with intent to do grievous bodily harm.' Judge Brett was concerned that 'this crime of stabbing was one that was becoming prevalent and must be put an end to'.

The judge sentenced Nappey to five years' hard labour, a punishment he hoped would deter others.

The Rawlinson family eventually moved away from Hambleton to Dewsbury, where John became a painter and his family went into the textile mills. The Nappey family remained in Hambleton, reunited after William was released from prison in 1875.

CHAPTER 28

A Great Outrage: Settle
1871

Christopher Wright had spent most of his life around Giggleswick, where he was born, and Langcliffe, where he died. He, and his wife Agnes, were beer sellers, helped by their two granddaughters, Annie and Agnes Atkinson. In January 1871, though both well into their seventies, they were making a good living since the Settle and Carlisle Railway was under construction and the navvies regularly came into the village to spend their wages, often at Wright's *Bay Horse Inn.*

On Monday 8 January they had several customers in their beerhouse. At about half past nine, Ellis Parker, also known as Nelson, arrived with his friend, Tom. They stayed drinking with friends until everyone got up to leave at about eleven o'clock. Parker and his friend remained behind.

The landlord asked Parker to leave, but the man refused, saying he wanted another gallon of ale. Though no ale was brought, the men refused to leave. Mrs Wright offered them sixpence to go, but though they took the money, they remained in the house.

At midnight, the granddaughter, Agnes, was sent out to Settle to fetch the constable, but though she searched the town she was unable to find one and returned to the beerhouse. There she found her grandmother waiting for her, along with a friend, Peter Smith. They all went inside together where Christopher Wright was still talking to Parker and trying to persuade him to leave. The girl told Parker that she had found the police and a constable was coming. Full of bravado, Parker replied that he 'didn't care' if three policemen came. He simply bolted the door and declared that if anyone came near him he 'would dash their brains out'.

Both the Wrights went and asked him to open the door, but Parker refused, pushing Mrs Wright out of the way and this time he lashed out at the old man, knocking him down, kicking and punching him violently a number of times. When Wright cried out, 'The Lord help me, I am killed,' Parker simply laughed at him. Smith and young Agnes carried the old man into the kitchen and eventually at 5 am, Parker and his friend left the house.

Dr William Altham was called in, treating Wright for severe bruises on his right leg, thigh and back, as well as wounds on his left arm and at the back of his head. Wright survived for almost a week but finally died from his injuries on the following Sunday. At the post-mortem, the doctor found bleeding into the skull and brain, and severe bruising of the kidneys which he considered were the cause of death, combined with shock to the system.

PC Taylor was informed of the death and, accompanied by Agnes Atkinson, went to an area known as Willy Wood where the railway navvies were living. She immediately identified Parker

Town Hall, Leeds. The author

who was arrested and taken back to the *Bay Horse* in Langcliffe. There the widow and Annie, the other granddaughter, also identified him as the murderer.

On the following day, 17 January, an inquest was held before T P Browne, deputy coroner where the jury brought in a verdict of manslaughter against Parker. He then appeared before the magistrates, J Birkbeck, Rev H J Swale and H Christie where it was noted that Parker was wearing clogs with iron bands round the sides, with which he had kicked the old man in the back and legs. The magistrates committed him for trial.

In April Parker appeared at the Leeds Assizes before Justice Brett. After hearing the statements from the family and surgeon, the jury quickly brought in a verdict of guilty of manslaughter. The judge was of the opinion that the event was closer to murder since:

The prisoner's conduct was as great an outrage as he had heard for many years and he could not sufficiently express the contempt he felt for the mode in which he [the prisoner] *had behaved himself on that night.*

Parker received five years' imprisonment. Agnes Wright stayed on in Langcliffe, though the *Bay Horse* lost its licence to sell beer.

CHAPTER 29

A Dreadful Murder: Sheffield 1865

Solomon Stenton was born in 1843, probably the illegitimate child of Elizabeth Stenton, aged seventeen. Her mother, Eliza Stenton (nee Hawksworth), could hardly throw the girl out since she too had been illegitimate, born to Eliza in 1827. By 1851 the girl was off working away from home and Solomon was living with his grandparents, Thomas, who was an ironstone miner, and Eliza. Just four years later, Thomas died, followed in 1856 by Solomon's mother. Eliza remarried in 1856 to William Drabwell (or Drabble) and Solomon continued to live with the couple.

Just a few years later, William too was dead and Eliza was left alone with her grandson, living in a small cottage at Green Head, Chapeltown.

Solomon worked as a labourer at the Thorncliffe Ironworks but he was frequently in trouble with the police, often appearing before magistrates for poaching, drunkenness and fighting. His ill temper was regularly taken out on his grandmother too. He was well known for his dissolute way of life, to the extent that his employers agreed to pay his wages to his grandmother, instead of to Solomon. She collected the money every alternate Friday.

On Friday 24 March 1865, Solomon was drinking in the *Coach and Horses*, whilst his grandmother went to Mortomley to collect his wages. At around eleven at night, she went to the *Coach and Horses*, as she usually did, to take her grandson home. This time however, Stenton swore at her and told her to go home or he would kill her. Eventually, Stenton agreed to go with the woman, and an acquaintance, William Hanson, left the pub with them. Almost immediately, Stenton punched his grandmother and kicked her as she fell to the ground. Hanson parted them and they walked on together for a short while before Stenton attacked the old woman again. Again, Hanson parted them and this time left them alone together, but watched them as they walked away. Barely twenty yards further on, Stenton knocked his grandmother down again, hitting her about the head and kicking her. Hanson ran to stop him. With the help of another onlooker, George Birkinshaw, he lifted her to the side of the road and stayed with her till she regained consciousness, muttering to her rescuers, 'I have got my death blow.' She set off again, on her own, but had barely walked through the Chapeltown toll bar when Stenton appeared and attacked her yet again, kicking her as she lay on the ground. Hanson pushed him away but it was too late. Dr Drew was sent for but the old lady was already dead.

Sergeant Tomlinson soon took Stenton into custody, taking him eventually to Hillsborough station. Inspector Bouchier took him to the Town Hall to appear before the magistrates on Saturday and he was remanded to the next assizes, charged with murder.

At the assizes in April before Justice Willes, Stenton seemed bewildered and unsure how to plead. 'I suppose I am guilty,' he said, 'I don't know what I didn't do.' The judge asked him if he had intended to kill his grandmother to which he replied, 'No.' 'Then that is not guilty,' he was told.

Mr Blackburn and Mr Gully prosecuted, whilst the defence was conducted by Mr Waddy. The evidence was heard from William Hanson, Eliza Elliot, landlady of the *Coach and Horses* and Dr Drew, who told the court:

> … *by order of the Coroner, I made a post-mortem examination of the body. The cause of death was the violence which I have heard described by the other witnesses.*

ALLEGED MURDER NEAR SHEFFIELD.—VERDICT
OF MANSLAUGHTER.
SOLOMON STENTON (20) labourer, was charged with the wilful murder of Eliza Drabble, his grandmother, at Chapeltown, near Sheffield on the 25th March. Mr. V. BLACKBURN and Mr. GULLY prosecuted; Mr. WADDY conducted the defence. On being asked whether he was

Headline, Leeds Mercury, *1865.*
Author's collection

Judge Willes pointed out that 'after that statement it was impossible for the Learned Counsel to resist a verdict of manslaughter'. Defence counsel replied that he 'would not address a single word to the jury'.

It hardly seemed necessary for the jury to rubber stamp the verdict, leaving only the sentencing to be decided on. Willes told Stenton:

You have brought your grandmother to a violent and shocking end by treatment such as I hope has horrified everybody in court... You have been found guilty of manslaughter and in passing sentence the Court must not overlook the fact that you are a person of bad character. The Court would be wrong, and it would be a bad lesson indeed if the Court did not pass upon you one of the most serious sentences known to the law and it is that you will be kept in penal servitude for twenty years.

CHAPTER 30

All for Avarice: Skipton
1846

hen John Rodda appeared before Judge Cresswell in York the lawyers had to tell the jury they would be hearing:

a charge so repugnant to the ordinary feelings of human nature that he must caution them against being prejudiced against the prisoner.

In April, John Rodda and his wife had been having problems with their eldest child, Mary, a little girl about eighteen months old. She had always been a sickly child but now seemed to be worse, probably because she was teething. On 16 April her mother had taken her to the doctor, who gave her medicine containing antimonial powder (also known as James' powder or fever powder) and calomel (a purgative), but she continued to be poorly. Neighbours popped in to see if they could help but the child continued crying. On 19 April, just after eight, Mary Guy left the house, sure the child was getting better since she had managed to eat a little porridge. When Ellen Holdsworth went round at nine o'clock the child was vomiting a dark frothy liquid that spilt onto its pinafore. They called the apothecary, Lawrence Bentham, who was not sure what the problem was but gave the child magnesia and this seemed to settle it. A short while later the vomiting started again, and by eleven o'clock the child was dead.

An inquest was held before Thomas Browne the coroner at the *Nag's Head Inn*, run by William Haworth.

Bentham explained his dealings with the child to the coroner, stating that there 'was a mucus of a dark livid colour about its mouth and chin' his impression being that someone had given the child sulphuric acid. He and William Bell, surgeon, performed the post-mortem which showed that the tongue and mouth 'looked parboiled' and the stomach was almost completely destroyed, so pulpy it fell apart.

The mother stated that she had been looking after the children all day. In the evening she had laid the two children on the father's knee while she went upstairs to make the bed. A few minutes later she heard the little girl scream and when she got downstairs she saw it was vomiting. She denied seeing any acid, saying it had only been given tea and porridge to her knowledge. The only people in the house at the time were the parents, neither of whom, by law, could testify for or against the other, but it was proved that the father had previously purchased a small bottle of oil of vitriol [sulphuric acid]. Since its effect was instantaneous and John Rodda was the only person in the room, he must have administered the liquid. If someone else was there and had given the liquid, then it must have been by his authority. Either way, he was guilty of murder.

Rodda said that he had neither bottle nor spoon nor anything else about him but the two children. He put Mary into a cradle when she began to vomit, then took her up again only when his wife came downstairs. He had got some stuff from a chemist but it was in a broken bottle so he threw it away.

The inquest jury brought in a verdict of murder and Rodda was sent to York to await trial.

In July Rodda came before Justice Cresswell. Defended by Mr Bliss, the prosecutors were Mr Hall and Mr Wasney. Rodda stated that he was thirty-three years old, a hawker of mats, living recently in Skipton and pleaded not guilty to the charge of wilful murder.

Mary Reader told the court she had been in conversation with Rodda ten days or so before the child's death. Rodda had told her that if Mary died he would get £2 10 shillings (£2.50) from a burial club for it and 'the sooner the child died the better as it was so sickly'.

Sarah Cooper, druggist (chemist) said that on 18 April, Rodda had bought one pennyworth of oil of vitriol from her for 'the destruction of bugs'. She had given him about a tablespoon of the liquid in a small bottle.

Thomas Lowcock, constable, produced the child's pinafore on which the vomit had burnt holes to the extent that the material crumbled on being touched. Evidence from the inquest was repeated but when Mr Bliss for the defence addressed the jury, he brought up the possibility that Mrs Cooper who 'neither weighed nor measured the oil of vitriol, could have given the prisoner some fluid from another bottle' therefore she was negligent. With regard to the money from the burial club, he thought it likely that people in poor circumstances when anticipating a death, would consider the manner they should inter the body and the expenses that would be incurred. The prisoner had stated openly that he'd get help from the club to defray the expenses, which was not the action of a guilty man. Rev Welsh, a priest from Keighley gave a character reference for Rodda, saying he had always known him as a kind father and humane man.

It took the jury an hour and a half to bring in a verdict of guilty. Judge Cresswell then informed him that 'the court must pronounce against him the most terrible sentence known to the law' that of hanging.

During his remaining days in prison, Rodda spent time with Rev T Billington, the Catholic Dean of York to whom he eventually made a full confession of his guilt, stating that avarice was his only motive for the killing. Rodda was hanged on Saturday 8 August at St George's Field, witnessed by a large crowd, many of whom were fellow Irish.

CHAPTER 31

Horrible Wife Murder: Skipton 1880

S uch was the Victorian fascination with murder that 'crowds of people wended their way to the scene of the crime' within hours of the fact becoming known.

Henry, a currier, and Margaret Blades had been married for eighteen years but things had never been easy between them. Nevertheless, they had produced thirteen children, though only four survived: Alfred (aged 15), Elizabeth (12), Arthur (9) and Sarah Ellen (7). Margaret had left home, but had returned to the family when they moved into the new lodgings in Russell Street, Middletown, Skipton, at the end of April. On Sunday 2 May rumours began to spread throughout the town that a terrible crime had been committed.

The couple were constantly arguing so when neighbours heard screaming on the Saturday night, they didn't really take much notice. The children heard and were afraid but were even more afraid of what their father would do to them if they got out of bed, so huddled in silence. The noises soon died down.

The next morning, Margaret was ill, Henry said. He refused to let his eldest daughter go in to see to her but looked after

HORRIBLE WIFE MURDER AT SKIPTON.

THE INQUEST.—VERDICT OF WILFUL MURDER.

CAPTURE OF THE MURDERER.

STATEMENT BY THE PRISONER.

About ten o'clock on Sunday night last a startling rumour became current that a dreadful wife murder had been committed in a house in

Headline, Craven Herald, *1880.*
Author's collection

them during the day, including cooking them a meal. He also took food upstairs to his wife. Only minutes later Elizabeth saw her father bring the plate down again and followed him into the kitchen, where he was tucking into the meal himself. She immediately told him that she did not believe her mother could have eaten the food so quickly. Henry glared at her and muttered that 'she had eaten what she wanted'. In alarm, Elizabeth asked if her mother was dead but Henry silenced her: 'Get on with thee; what's tha talking that silly talk for?'

The pair spent the day dodging each other, Elizabeth trying to get into the bedroom to see her mother and Henry keeping her away. She did see her father tying a rope to a hook in the kitchen and managed to snatch a look at a slate on which her father had written 'Dear Friends, I hope you will not let my poor children go to the workhouse ...' but that was all she saw before her father knocked it from her hands.

Later Henry sent his children away from the house, leaving it himself for a short while. Elizabeth went to her Aunt Lizzie, her mother's sister, and the pair returned to see what was going on. As they approached the front door, Henry walked out at the back door and ran away.

Inside, Elizabeth and her aunt, together with a neighbour, Ellen Dawson, went in and found Margaret Blades dead. Police and the local doctor, Dr Wylie, were called. They concluded Margaret had been strangled and began the search for her husband.

On the Monday evening an inquest was held at the *Unicorn Inn* before T P Brown, the coroner. The jury consisted of William Cowman (foreman), John Schofield, Thomas Wilkinson, George Severs, Joseph Septimus Baxter, Henry Howarth, Cornelius Hawkins, Thomas Manby, William Lawson, Samuel Thornton, Thomas Black, Lawrence Hargreaves and Fred Alderson.

Elizabeth told the jury all that had happened the previous night, saying she had heard her parents arguing. It was the evidence of a neighbour, Elizabeth Fagan, wife of the local plumber that proved pivotal. She said she had seen Henry the previous week, when he had been searching for his wife, who was regularly out drinking. He had muttered threats against

Unicorn Inn, *Skipton.* The author

his wife and when Mrs Fagan saw Mrs Blades, around eleven o'clock on the Saturday night, the woman had asked to stay with the Fagans as, she said, she daren't go home, as her husband would kill her. That same Saturday night, Mrs Fagan saw Henry looking for his wife and saying, 'I will do for her tonight.'

The slate, which young Elizabeth Blades had tried to see, was read out in court:

> *Dear Friends, I hope you will never let my poor childer go to the workhouse, for they will do some one some good. No finer children born in the world than them for working so I hope to the Lord you will do your best to them and I think they do the same to you. It is heart-breaking to leave them, but we must part, so hope it will be a warning to you all not to get the same fate as this; so I hope you will do your best to my childering for it is hard work parting with them. They are standing over me the time I am writing so I will say no more for my heart is bursting to see them.*

On the envelope was written:

I cannot live any longer the way things is going on, so I will bid you all good bye, hoping to live in peace for it has been a troublesome life and I hope all friends will look over it. So I remain your sorrowful heart, good by to all.

The jury did raise the question of insanity, but the coroner told them it was not for them to consider. They then had no choice but to bring in a verdict of wilful murder against Henry Blades.

Sergeant Chisholme, together with PCs Whipp, Whittaker and Acton set off for Bradley, where Henry's parents lived. Leaving Whipp to watch the house, the others searched outbuildings and the surrounding countryside. Finally, in the early hours of Wednesday morning they found a man lying in the hay. He stated his name as 'William Smith' of Keighley but Chisholme arrested him anyway, charging him with vagrancy and taking him into Skipton, sure he would be identified as Blades. Sure enough, on the outskirts of the town, Blades admitted that he was the man they wanted and was immediately charged with his wife's murder.

Rather than causing a stir by taking him to the Town Hall, Blades was brought before J B Dewhurst at the police station. Since the inquest had already been held and Superintendent Exton had a coroner's warrant for Blades it was a simple matter for him to be remanded in custody until the following week. Blades was immediately put on 'suicide watch' whilst in prison and was eventually sent for trial at the assizes.

Henry Blades seems to have had many friends and sympathisers in Skipton. His former employer, Thomas Herrington, wrote to the *Craven Herald* stating that he was a good worker and 'extremely fond of his children' but whose life had been 'fearfully embittered by an unfaithful drunken wife'. A fund was raised to provide for Henry's defence.

In August, Blades appeared before Justice Bowen at the Town Hall, Leeds. The prosecution was undertaken by Messrs Lockwood, Fenwick and Kershaw, whilst the defence, funded by the contributions of the local populace, was undertaken by

Messrs Tindal Atkinson and Slingsby. The jury consisted of: James Ainsworth, Thomas Bentley, William Haverson, James Crabtree, Benjamin Heaton, Thomas Downs, Thomas Metcalfe, Benjamin Jackson, Walter Parkinson, Henry Gibson, John Booth and William Hampson.

Henry Blades pleaded not guilty to murder.

Henry listened again to the prosecution explaining the events of the night of 2 May. The only time he showed any emotion was when his daughter took the stand to describe what had happened. She also confirmed that her father regularly had to go out searching for her mother and, in fact, Elizabeth herself had gone with her father during the early part of Saturday evening looking for her mother. She had returned home when it got dark and her father continued alone.

Other neighbours too came forward to give evidence. Patience Pullen said she was in her sitting room on the Saturday night when she heard Margaret Blades come home, about 11 o'clock at night. About half an hour later, Henry Blades arrived home and shortly after that she heard groaning or choking noises coming from the Blades' bedroom. She heard Elizabeth cry out 'Father don't' and Blades reply, 'If you don't make less noise, I'll kill you.'

Sergeant Collins described finding the body in the house, describing the marks on each side of her windpipe and the finding of the rope hanging on a hook in the back kitchen. The defence questioned him closely about these marks, since at the inquest his statement only mentioned one mark on the left of the throat. The sergeant insisted that he had spoken of two marks but was at a loss to explain why this did not appear in his statement. The defence also asked about who was in the town on the night of the murder, making much of the fact that there were a number of soldiers in the area.

Dr William Wylie described Margaret Blades as having a long mark on the left side of the neck and no other marks on her neck but did see a large mark on her right shoulder blade, which looked like the imprint of a boot. Another, similar, mark was found on the right hip. The rest of the body he found to be healthy, but stated that he found no traces of alcohol in her stomach. He gave the cause of death as strangulation.

Again the defence tried hard to mitigate the circumstances, suggesting that the woman had not, in fact, been strangled since this would have created bruising on both sides of the neck, but that it was possible that her husband might have grabbed hold of her and then fallen, causing sudden and violent pressure on the larynx. The doctor did eventually agree that this was possible and that she could have lived for half an hour or an hour after such pressure. Under cross-examination, he stated that the pressure on the larynx would have to be long and continued, though he could not account for the murmuring noises heard after the supposed assault. When asked about the lack of alcohol in the stomach, he admitted that this could have been 'due to the rapid absorption of drink in a dead body.'

Unusually, Blades elected to make a statement to the jury before their decision, and the judge allowed it. Blades explained how he had spent the day searching for his wife, in between providing breakfast and dinner for their children. Margaret had been and sold some of their possessions, and then, it appears, spent most of the money on drink. When she had finally returned home, she had refused to say where she had been or who she'd been with. He tackled her about the lack of food for the family, and she replied that she didn't care about the children, taunting him with the fact that one of them wasn't even his child anyway. When he went to look in her pocket for money, she flew at him, punching him with her fists and finally attacking him with a brass candlestick. He removed that from her grasp but lost his temper and grabbed her by the side of the neck. In the struggle, they fell back on the bed, Henry landing on top of his wife, catching her in her side with his knee. This knocked her senseless for a while, but when she came round he made her some tea and she seemed a little better. By four in the morning she became worse and finally ceased breathing. Henry panicked, not knowing what to do, until his sister-in-law arrived, when he ran away from the house. He denied using a rope on his wife, saying he'd intended to take his own life, but then changed his mind. He also denied making any serious threats against his wife, insisting that even if he had used such words, they were simply an expression, not a statement of intent. 'I never thought to kill my wife … my passion got the better of me and I did not know what I did.'

The question for the jury was to decide whether the case was wilful murder or whether there were mitigating circumstances:

> *If the prisoner killed the woman with the intention of killing her, then it was murder, but if he killed her not with any preconceived notion, then it was not murder but manslaughter.*

The judge summed up the evidence, commenting on the character of the man who had moved house, simply to please the woman and bring her back to the family:

> *One fact was patent, namely that the woman was not throttled, otherwise there would have been distinct marks … the prisoner was a man who was fond of his children and would have loved his wife if she would have let him.*

The *Craven Herald* goes on to say that 'at this point the prisoner became deeply affected, as were many other people in Court, including one or two of the jurymen'.

After the summing up, a number of people were called to give a character witness for the prisoner.

Thomas Herrington had trained Blades in his occupation as a currier and employed him after he had finished his apprenticeship. Herrington described the man as 'quiet, steady and well-disposed'. Robert Currer, postmaster at Bradley had known Blades all his life and said he was 'indisposed to be quarrelsome'. Francis Addyman had also known Blades for many years as the prisoner had worked not just for Addyman but for his father as well. John Bramley was a former employer who stated that Mrs Blades had often come to the works just to annoy Henry, who was a very steady and hard-working man.

The judge then told the jury they must make their decision, informing them that they should place no particular importance on what Blades did after the event since this was probably the result of despair. The crucial evidence was that of Mrs Pullen since, together with the doctor's statement, it suggested that Mrs Blades could have lived for some time afterwards but that the pressure on her neck was considerable. The judge stressed that this dispelled the notion that manslaughter was an option. Taking a life was murder whether premeditated or not if the violence that caused the death was intended to do grievous bodily harm. No provocation, which could reduce the sentence, had been proved.

After barely fifteen minutes' deliberation, the jury returned a verdict of manslaughter.

Christ Church, Skipton. The author

Judge Bowen described Blades action as 'a most brutal crime' and he was 'guilty of unmanly, wicked violence...' As a result he was sentenced to twenty years' penal servitude.

Margaret Blades was interred in the burial ground at Christ Church, Skipton. The two little girls, Elizabeth and Sarah Ellen, went to live with their Aunt Lizzie, her husband, John Chester and their children. The two boys seem to have found themselves lodgings in Skipton. Alfred was only nine years old but was already employed as a mill hand, whilst Arthur, at only sixteen, was a weaver and became the head of his household. What seems unusual is that Arthur was present in the house during the events of 2 May but was not called as a witness. Instead the police called on his younger sister, Elizabeth. No reason was given for Arthur's possible evidence being ignored.

CHAPTER 32

Shocking Wife Murder: Thurlstone 1867

On Saturday 9 February, at the *Crystal Palace Inn*, Thurlstone a coroner's inquest met before Thomas Taylor, coroner for the Honour of Pontefract.

In 1857 Joseph Jubb, alias Moss, a farm labourer, married Elizabeth Jubb. There was an extensive Jubb family in that area at the time and many of the family lived nearby. In fact, Elizabeth's mother, Hannah, lived next door to the family and saw her daughter a number of times during the week.

On Thursday 31 January, Elizabeth visited her mother but did not complain of feeling ill, despite the fact that she was in the latter stages of pregnancy. The following week she sent her daughter, Mary who was seven years old, to fetch Hannah. Joseph Jubb was in the house but made no comment, merely handed over a bottle of medicine, which Hannah gave to her

Crystal Palace, *Thurlstone*. The author

daughter. Elizabeth told her mother that she had been doing some washing for William Wood and had fallen against the tub. Now she complained of a pain in her stomach. Hannah stopped for over an hour, helping her daughter to bed and took the washing home to finish. Whilst there she heard her daughter say to Joseph, 'Well old devil thou wants to kill what's in me.' Joseph replied, 'That's true, I do.'

She went back on a number of occasions that day as her daughter's condition worsened. At half past six on Thursday morning Hannah went again. She thought that Elizabeth knew who she was but could not be certain, as the woman was almost delirious. By ten o'clock she was dead.

George Frederick Leigh, surgeon, of Penistone, conducted a post-mortem, when he found extensive bruising down her right side, with the obvious marks of nails from a boot all down her left leg. On investigating further he found that the placenta had separated, causing internal bleeding. The cause of this separation was external blows, or possibly a fall.

The local police sergeant, George Batty, stated that he had been present at the post-mortem and had seen Leigh take a boot belonging to Joseph Jubb and compare it to the nail marks on the deceased's leg. They matched perfectly.

Despite this, the coroner's jury brought in a verdict of 'died from injuries received, cause unknown'.

The police, however, were not happy with that and continued their investigations, taking many statements from neighbours until they amassed sufficient evidence to charge Joseph with his wife's murder. He appeared before Barnsley's police court, the prosecution being led by Thomas Greensit Hamer.

The witnesses drew a picture of a very unhappy life. Joseph was frequently drunk and generally violent. Elizabeth almost always had some marks of violence about her, and had her arm broken on one occasion. Another time a number of front teeth had been kicked out.

Hannah Dransfield, a widow who lived next door to the Jubbs, stated that on the 31 January, Elizabeth Jubb had come

Headline, Leeds Mercury, *1867.*
Author's collection

SHOCKING WIFE MURDER IN
YORKSHIRE.
Yesterday, at the Barnsley Police court, the
itting magistrates were occupied for several hours investi-

running into her house, with Joseph chasing her to try to get some money off his wife. He returned home and later Elizabeth followed him, accompanied by Mrs Dransfield. Elizabeth then accused her husband of kicking her and showed her neighbour the marks. Joseph remarked that he had been lame long enough and now it was her turn. Elizabeth also accused him of kicking her 'on the lower part of her body' and again showed the marks. Mrs Dransfield continued to look after Elizabeth over the next few days, since the woman was so ill she was unable to nurse her other little child.

When Joseph went to tell her that Elizabeth had died, Mrs Dransfield said, 'Now Joe, what have you done?' to which he replied, 'It's a bad job.' They went together to view the body and Joseph was concerned that people would say he had killed her. He asked his neighbour not to say anything against him and he 'would reward thee for it and see thou never has to go out washing again.' He even offered to knock the two houses into one so they could live as man and wife! Despite his continuing to press her not to say anything, Mrs Dransfield told the court that she had continually been disturbed by his violence and had even got out of bed on a number of occasions to throw stones at their door and get him to stop beating his wife.

Ann Woodcock (whose statement was read out in court as she was ill and couldn't attend) and Mary Ann Marshall both confirmed that they had seen Elizabeth just before her death and seen the blood on her nightdress and the bed. They had also seen a massive bruise along the side of her abdomen.

Together with other, similar, statements from neighbours and the details from the post-mortem, the evidence was sufficient for the Barnsley magistrates to send Jubb to Leeds for trial on an indictment of manslaughter.

He appeared before Justice Lush at the Spring Assizes. Mr Shaw and Mr Waddy prosecuted. This time, Mrs Dransfield also told the court that Elizabeth had told her that she had got up to open the door for her husband when he arrived home very late and the worse for drink. She had gone back to bed but he had demanded his supper. She pointed to it but he decided it was not good enough. He went up to the bed and 'thrashed her' as she lay there, cowering under the bedclothes to avoid two black eyes and the loss of yet more teeth. He then turned on the furniture and took his temper out on a clothes horse covered in clothes Elizabeth had taken in to wash. She got up to prevent him and he immediately began kicking her abdomen, thighs and back. She also said she had frequently heard his children scream as well as their mother.

Not for the first time, Jubb shouted out in court, 'Thou hast told some of the most confounded lies, Hannah, all the way through.' The judge intervened on a number of occasions as Jubb shouted at the various witnesses and threatened to have him taken back to the cells.

Superintendent Fisher pointed out that Jubb had told him that Elizabeth had fallen and he had, in fact, done all he could to help her, but the surgeons were adamant that the bruises were such that they could not have been caused by a fall, particularly the ones which showed nail marks from the boots.

Jubb then addressed the jury on his own behalf, stating that he had only kicked his wife once and that the other, worse, bruises were caused by a fall. The jury did not believe him and brought in a verdict of guilty.

The judge commended the jury and told Jubb that his crime was manslaughter 'on the very verge of murder'. Jubb was imprisoned for twenty years.

Elizabeth Jubb was buried in St John's church, Penistone on 9 February 1867.

St John's church, Penistone. The author

CHAPTER 33

Determined Suicide: Wakefield 1847

t the beginning of February, an event took place that 'created a great sensation in the neighbourhood and whereby two respectable families have been thrown into a state of the deepest distress'.

For the past three years, George Hampson, aged twenty-five, had been 'paying his addresses' to Susannah Morton, the twenty-one-year-old daughter to Elizabeth Morton, a widow. George was the son of George Hampson a whitesmith in Wakefield, a well-respected craftsman. The lad had everything to look forward to: good prospects working in his father's business and marriage to the girl of his choice, described by the *Leeds Mercury* as 'a fine figure and very pretty'.

On the last Friday in January, Hampson went, as usual, to Susannah's house. She was not feeling well and had sent for her sister, Fanny, to come but by the time the girl arrived, Susannah was better, though still a little faint. At about ten o'clock, Fanny persuaded the pair to go out for a walk with her to get some fresh air. After walking around the St John's area for a while, Fanny left to go home and the young couple returned to Susannah's house. Her brother, John, left them alone together when he retired to bed and that was the last time anyone saw them alive.

The following morning, two coats, a hat, bonnet, shawl and boa were found on the banks of the Barnsley Canal near a bridge, about a mile and a half from where Susannah lived. An immediate search was made and it was not long before the two bodies were found. The bodies were tied together with four handkerchiefs 'which must have been fastened by Hampson, as the knots were behind the young woman'.

In Hampson's pocket the searchers found a pistol loaded with ball, two bullets and some powder and caps. In Susannah's pockets they found 'a soft substance like paste...which is supposed to be poison'.

The *Leeds Mercury* reported:

> *What tends to make the affair more mysterious is the total inability of anyone to find a reason for the commission of such a rash act. There were no marks of violence on either of the bodies or anything to lend to the belief that either of them had come to their deaths by unfair means.*

An inquest was held before Thomas Lee, coroner, where eventually the jury returned a verdict of:

> *Found drowned, without any marks of violence, but how, or by what means they got into the canal there is no evidence to show.*

The lovers were buried together in All Saints' church, Wakefield.

All Saints' church (the Cathedral), Wakefield.
The author

Sources

Chapter 1
The Times
Wakefield Journal and West Riding Herald
Leeds Mercury
Dorothy Thompson, *The Chartists*, Temple Smith, 1984

Chapter 2
Huddersfield Weekly Examiner, 1867–68
Leeds Mercury, 1861–68
Coroner's Inquest Report, WYAS, Wakefield
Wakefield Express, 1867–68
Census records, 1861 and 1881

Chapter 3
Leeds Mercury, 1870
Huddersfield Examiner, 1870

Chapter 4
Dewsbury Reporter, 1863
Leeds Mercury, 1863

Chapter 5
1861 Census, Batley
Huddersfield Weekly Examiner, 1863
Dewsbury Reporter, 1863
Leeds Mercury, 1863

Chapter 6
CD. J Chambers, *Death & Transportation Yorkshire*, 1830–1839
Leeds Mercury, 1837
Stillingfleet parish register (IGI)

Chapter 7
Leeds Mercury, 1844

Chapter 8
The Times, 1848
Leeds Mercury, 1848

Chapter 9
Leeds Mercury, 1837 and 1838
CD. J Chambers, *Death & Transportations Yorkshire, 1830–1839*

Chapter 10
Leeds Mercury, 1877
Halifax Weekly Courier, 1877
Brighouse News, 1877
Lightcliffe Cemetery records
Census records, 1861–81

Chapter 11
Taylor notebooks, C493 K 2 1 K29, WYAS
The Times, 1869
Leeds Mercury, 1869

Chapter 12
Census records, 1851 -1881
Huddersfield Weekly Examiner, 1871

Chapter 13
C493 K2 1 116 Taylor notebooks no 116
Census records, 1871
Dewsbury Reporter, 1873

Chapter 14
Leeds Mercury, 1828
CD. *Criminal Chronology*

Chapter 15
Huddersfield Weekly Examiner, 1866
Leeds Mercury, 1866
The Times, 1866

Chapter 16
The Times, 1896
Huddersfield Examiner, 1896
Leeds Mercury, 1896
Census records
Civil Registration records

Chapter 17
Leeds Mercury, 1870
Goole Times, 1870
Census records, 1861–1871

Chapter 18
Huddersfield Weekly Examiner, 1858
Census returns, 1841 and 1851
The Times online, 1858
Criminal Chronology of York Castle
Leeds Mercury, 1858

Chapter 19
The Times 1868
Huddersfield Weekly Examiner 1868
Thomas Taylor notebooks C493 2 1 29 no 1473

Chapter 20
Huddersfield Examiner, 1866
Census records

Chapter 21
Huddersfield Examiner, 1888
Leeds Mercury, 1888

Chapter 22
Leeds Mercury, 1841
The Times, 1841
Criminal Chronology of York Castle
Census records, 1841

Chapter 23
Leeds Mercury, 1847

Chapter 24
The Times, 1837
Leeds Mercury, 1837
Northern Star and Leeds General Advertiser, 1837
Parish Registers: Pontefract, Ferry Fryston, Knottingley

Chapter 25
Leeds Mercury, 1791–3
Morning Herald, 1791
Morning Post and Daily Advertiser, 1791–3

Evening Post, 1791–3
Criminal Chronology of York Castle CD
IGI

Chapter 26
Criminal Chronology of York Castle
The Times, 1850
Manchester Times, 1850

Chapter 27
Leeds Mercury, 1870
Goole Times, 1870
Census Records, 1851–1881

Chapter 28
Craven Pioneer, 1871
Huddersfield Examiner, 1871
http://www.langcliffe.net/Murder.htm

Chapter 29
Leeds Mercury, 1865
Census records, 1841–61

Chapter 30
Leeds Intelligencer, 1846
Leeds Mercury, 1846
Hull Packet and East Riding Times, 1846
Criminal Chronology of York Castle

Chapter 31
Craven Herald, 1880
Leeds Mercury, 1880
Census, 1881

Chapter 32
Leeds Mercury, 1867
Census, 1851–71

Index

Places

NB For smaller place-names please see nearest main urban area eg Sheffield (Tankersely)